Family of Origin Applications in Clinical Supervision

Family of Origin Applications in Clinical Supervision

Carlton E. Munson, DSW
Editor

The Haworth Press
New York

Family of Origin Applications in Clinical Supervision has also been published as *The Clinical Supervisor,* Volume 2, Number 2, Summer 1984.

The Haworth Press, Inc., 28 East 22 Street, New York, NY 10010

Library of Congress Cataloging in Publication Data
Main entry under title:

Family of origin applications in clinical supervision.

    Published also as v. 2, no. 2 of the Clinical supervisor.
    Includes bibliographies.
    1. Family psychotherapy—Study and teaching. 2. Psychotherapists—Supervision of.
3. Family. I. Munson, Carlton E.
RC488.5.F326 1984   616.89'156   84-9017
ISBN 0-86656-287-7

Family of Origin Applications in Clinical Supervision

The Clinical Supervisor
Volume 2, Number 2

CONTENTS

Family of Origin
Applications in
Clinical Supervision

Editor's Comments

When I accepted the editorship of *The Clinical Supervisor* and was encouraged to develop several thematic special issues, I knew immediately I wanted to devote a special issue to the use of family of origin material in clinical supervision. The use of family of origin material in practice and supervision is fairly widespread (reliable statistics on the exact amount of its application are not available), but very little has been published on the topic. For supervisors and practitioners interested in the use of family of origin material, it has been difficult to locate theoretical and practical literature. In developing this special issue, it is our hope that supervisors will now have some guidelines and practical examples available for use in their supervisory practice. It is our intention that this issue will serve as "a statement of the art" on family of origin in supervision.

This special issue has taken over one year to prepare, and I want to thank all the contributors for their work and patience. All of the articles, except the one by Shirley Braverman, were prepared as original pieces for this special issue. Braverman's article appeared in the *Canadian Journal of Psychiatry,* and we want to express appreciation to that journal for permission to reprint her excellent article. The lead article by Michael Kerr from The Family Center at Georgetown University Hospital provides an overview of family of origin theory from the origins to the most current thinking about its application. Kerr's paper serves as a foundation for all the other articles that deal directly with supervision and family of origin material.

It is our hope that our readers will find this special issue helpful.

Carlton E. Munson

Theoretical Base for Differentiation of Self in One's Family of Origin

Michael E. Kerr

Murray Bowen's presentation of his paper, *Toward The Differentiation of a Self In One's Own Family* (1972), at a national meeting of family therapists in March 1967 had an impact that still reverberates throughout the family movement. In the paper Bowen described his effort toward being more of a self in relationship to his family of origin. The presentation actually had two effects. It not only communicated what he had done in his family, but it also established a position for him in the then rapidly developing family movement. This position was established by two clear implications in his paper; namely, that theory was an essential base for the conduct of psychotherapy and that effective therapy was contingent on the therapist's ability to look at his or her emotional functioning. Many accolades were showered on Bowen for his pioneering work, but in the years since 1967, many misconceptions have arisen about his theory and its application to family of origin. This paper will attempt to eliminate some of these misconceptions.

HISTORICAL BACKGROUND

Numerous clinical experiences and research developments contributed to the eventual theoretical understanding of the family of origin. Focus on the family of origin in therapy became possible only through acquiring this theoretical knowledge. Bowen's experience at the Menninger Clinic, a multigenerational research project conducted at Georgetown, and the refinement of the concept of a triangle all were particularly important to the understanding of extended family.

Michael E. Kerr, M.D., is Director of Training, The Family Center, Georgetown University Hospital.

3

Bowen trained and worked at the Menninger Clinic between 1946 and 1954. It was the occasions that necessitated his being away from Menninger's for brief periods that provided some of his first insights into the nature of emotional systems. A particularly difficult concept to grasp in systems theory is what it means to be in good emotional contact with a relationship system and, at the same time, not be an emotional participant in that system. This is frequently referred to as staying "outside" the system or as not getting "caught" in the system. Staying outside the system is frequently misinterpreted to mean being emotionally distant. Bowen's first inkling as to what it was like to be outside a system resulted from the realization that he could think more clearly and objectively about the people at Menninger's when he was away. The physical distance and absence of stories about who did what to whom and what was wrong with so-and-so seemed to be what permitted more objectivity. Despite considerable determination, Bowen found it difficult to retain this objectivity after he was back at Menninger's more than a few days. It usually took another trip away for him to even realize objectivity had been lost. Getting caught in the system could start with a derogatory or idealized remark made to him by one staff member about another who was not present. When Bowen later encountered the person about whom he had heard the remark, his thinking, feelings, and behavior toward that person were somewhat altered by the story he had heard. It was such an automatic process, it was difficult to escape. This is, obviously, not a phenomenon peculiar to Bowen or the Menninger system. It occurs everywhere. The awareness of the importance of this kind of phenomenon led Bowen to think of groups of people as comprising an emotional field. The emotional field regulates, to varying degrees, the attitudes and behavior of the group members toward one another. This concept of the group as an emotional field later proved applicable to the relationship system in the extended family.

Bowen left the Menninger Clinic to begin a research project at N.I.M.H. in 1954. The family research conducted there between 1954 and 1959 made a major contribution to the development of the basic concepts in family systems theory. The observations of the nuclear families that lived on the wards, for example, formed the basic elements in the concept of *nuclear family emotional process.* Bowen transferred his family research to Georgetown in 1959 and soon thereafter began a new project of assembling extensive multigenerational histories on a number of families. He believed that the emotional patterns that had been defined in the nuclear families of the N.I.M.H. project were identical to patterns that existed in nuclear families back through the generations. The multigenerational research was undertaken to confirm this hypothesis.

As the multigenerational research progressed, Bowen became intrigued with the new perspective it provided. The present emotional functioning of a family was more understandable when viewed in the context of its multigenerational past. Bowen found himself in the peculiar position of being a family researcher who knew a lot more about other people's families than about his own family. This realization was a stimulus for him to undertake similar research on his own family. It is important to emphasize that the goal of this early research was to learn about families and not to treat them. As others became interested in the family of origin, the importance of this increased understanding was frequently lost in the zeal to do therapy.

The first appreciation that patterns of interaction in a family could be conceptualized as triangles occurred during the N.I.M.H. research. It was not until about 1964, however, that Bowen saw the operation of triangles in the kind of microscopic detail necessary to allow application of the concept to his own family.

The activity of triangles is governed by an emotional process. Until this process can be accurately observed in oneself and others, triangles have little more than geometric meaning. Because of the necessity of being able to observe the emotional reactions that drive triangles, reading and lectures have limited value for learning about them. Understanding triangles, however, is critical to the approach to family of origin. Triangles are the molecules of emotional systems. They permit one to see order in the midst of seemingly chaotic interactions.

The Menninger experience, the multigenerational research at Georgetown, and the development of the concept of triangles were critical factors in the eventual defining of a method to work on oneself in the context of existing relationships with family of origin. In addition to this new learning about human behavior, focus on family of origin also depended on unlearning some old concepts about behavior. Bowen was trained in psychoanalytic theory. Learning to think systems in reference to human behavior meant giving up the explanations psychoanalytic concepts had provided. Psychoanalytic theory had to be viewed as a set of assumptions rather than a body of facts. It also had to be seen as *descriptive,* rather than as a theory that could *account* for human behavior. Everyone attempting to move toward a systems way of thinking faces the same task of unlearning individual concepts that Bowen faced. While mental health professionals usually receive less formal training in psychoanalytic concepts than in the past, these concepts continue to be a major influence on thinking about human behavior. Psychoanalytic theory and other concepts of behavior based on the study of the individual still permeate scientific journals, literature, the arts and the media. The human tendency in emotionally charged atmospheres is to focus primarily on factors perceived to exist within the individual to explain behavior. The tensions of a group are blamed on the behavior of certain individuals in the group. Human beings do this in families, social groups, and on the national and international level. Our own part in whatever occurs around us is usually overlooked. The higher the tension level, the greater the tendency to diagnose others. Tunnel vision seems built into us and is only reinforced by professional training.

Bowen puzzled over how little use psychoanalytic training had for helping him deal with the people who were closest and most important to him. It was a dictum of the psychoanalytic orientation that one's relatives and close friends be referred to another therapist for their problems. Psychoanalytic theory does not provide the theoretical base for working on oneself in relationship to one's own family. Bowen could easily apply labels such as hysteric, obsessive, alcoholic, etc. to various family members, but such a skill contributes little to understanding and improving family relationships. As his clinical family research progressed, however, Bowen became intrigued with the possibility of applying the new theoretical understanding of families to his own family. He wondered if it would be possible to be in the midst of his family of origin and remain outside the emotional field.

After many unsuccessful attempts at this over a period of about ten years, a trip home in August 1966 was unusually productive. A clearer understanding of triangles and more freedom from the tendency to diagnose others made the difference. The August 1966 trip was at a time of fairly intense emotional turmoil in his family so much planning preceded the visit. During the week at home, he was able to make good emotional contact with each family member, listen to all the stories, and still not get caught in the emotional system. He had as much emotional neutrality when he left the system as when he entered it. Emotional neutrality is another way of describing being outside the system. It is the ability to see both sides of relationship issues and to be neutral about the fact that things are the way they are in one's family. Bowen considered the most important success of the trip the validation that theoretical concepts such as the triangle and differentiation of self were applicable to the family of origin. The theory was demonstrated to be an adequate guide through the maze of relationships and potential emotional obstacles in the extended family.

Six months later Bowen presented the theoretical basis for what he had done in his family to a national meeting of family therapists. Working on self in relationship to family of origin quickly became the central focus of training family therapists at Georgetown. Sufficient experience with trainees attempting this in their own families had accumulated by 1971 to suggest that it was an unusually effective form of therapy. During the 1970s, other therapists around the country became interested in family of origin, but they approached it from a different theoretical orientation. Many had understood Bowen to be applying some kind of new technical maneuvers with family of origin and did not grasp the theoretical underpinnings on which his approach was based.

During the 1950s, Bowen, like most others, had recommended personal psychoanalysis to young therapists as the best available method for working on their own problems and enhance their clinical effectiveness. Around 1960, based on the growing understanding of differentiation of self, he started to recommend therapists choose family therapy with their spouse instead of psychoanalysis. The goal was to work on differentiation of self in relationship to one's spouse rather than to work out a transference relationship with an analyst. After 1967, Bowen considered working on differentiation of self in relationship to one's parents as the approach with the most potential. One fascinating thing that emerged was that people who focused on their parental families and never had a therapy session involving their spouse reported significant changes in their nuclear family relationships. The perspective gained through working on self in family of origin carried over into the nuclear family. In fact, change seemed to occur faster in the nuclear family when the nuclear family was not the primary focus of one's efforts.

Bowen now considers establishing the fact that people can work on emotional maturity through efforts at directly resolving attachments to their original family to be one of Georgetown's most important contributions. Therapy sessions four times a week to build a transference were no longer necessary. The therapist became a kind of "coach" to a person's working on the ultimate transference with their parents. Some have challenged the claim of Bowen and his associates that people can achieve the level of objectivity necessary to change in relationship to their own families. People *can* achieve this level of objectivity, and systems theory has provided the necessary lens.

THEORETICAL PRINCIPLES

The basic theoretical assumption that guides an effort toward a better level of differentiation of self in relationship to one's family of origin is that *every person has some degree of unresolved emotional attachment to their parental family.* This is as true of people in their eighties as of people in their twenties. This unresolved attachment to family of origin parallels one's level of differentiation of self. To understand the relationship between differentiation and the unresolved attachment to one's family, it is first necessary to examine the concept of differentiation in some detail.

The concept of differentiation describes two distinct, but closely interrelated processes. It describes something that occurs within people and it describes something about the way people function in relationships.

As it pertains to a process within people, differentiation refers to an individual's capacity to be *aware* of the difference between their intellectually determined and their emotionally determined functioning, and to have some *choice* about the degree to which each type of functioning governs their behavior. This capacity is best evaluated when a person is relating to a highly anxious environment. It is in those situations that the tendency for emotionality to override thinking is the greatest. Subtle differences exist between people in regards to the capacity to separate thinking and emotion, so thinking in terms of a continuum is a useful way to conceptualize differentiation. At one end of the continuum are the most undifferentiated people and at the other end are the more differentiated ones. Bowen reserved the optimum or highest levels of differentiation as something the human might eventually attain through continued evolution. There is an important distinction to be made between *basic* and *functional* levels of differentiation. People emerge from their families with a relatively fixed basic level of self or differentiation. This basic level has become built-in to the person and is not altered by relationships or other environmental circumstances. It is non-negotiable in relationships. Functional level of differentiation, on the other hand, refers to an *apparent* higher or lower level of self that is contingent on environmental factors. An example of this is one person bolstering his emotional strength and sense of well-being by relating to another person as if the other is less adequate or inferior. The other person plays out the opposite side in this process. This process is unrelated to sexual differences. It can occur in any relationship in which people have emotional significance to each other. The end result is that one person *functions* with a higher level of differentiation than the other, even though each has the same *basic* level of self. The lower the level of basic differentiation, the greater is this tendency for people to "borrow" self from others to shore up their own functioning. People can also borrow self from institutions, social causes, and a variety of other affiliations. Bowen has also used the term *pseudoself* to describe this artificial inflation or deflation of self. It is not a question of some people doing it and others not doing it. It is a question, rather, of some people doing it more than others.

Differentiation also describes the way people function in relationships. In this sense, it refers to the variation between people in terms of their ability to maintain emotional autonomy in a relationship system. This, again, is best evaluated in an anxious system where there is a greater tendency for people to both override each other and to be repelled by each other. Emotional autonomy is not to be confused with a *denial* of one's emotional need for others. Denial can result in a pseudo independent posture toward others and relates to a lack of emotional autonomy. The higher the level of emotional autonomy or differentiation of self, the greater the capacity to be in close contact with emotionally significant others without having one's thinking, emotions, and behavior governed by those relationships. Again, it is not a matter of whether one's behavior should or should not be regulated by the emotional environment, but it is a matter of retaining the capacity to have a choice about it. Another facet of differentiation in relationships is that the higher the level of self, the greater the ability not only to maintain a self in relationship to others, but also to permit others to be themselves. Another way of saying this is that the lower the level of differentiation, the more intense a person's emotional need for important others to think, feel, and behave in certain ways. The more undifferentiated the person, the more his life is dictated by the emotional aspects of relationships and of the environment. The greater the undifferentiation, the more thinking is undefined and awash in emotionality. The person becomes a rudderless ship, continually buffeted, for better and for worse, by the emotional winds that surround him. The greater the undifferentiation, the greater the tendency for a person to be either unable to function without an intense relationship or unable to function when in an intense relationship. Serious schizophrenia represents an extreme of this process, but is clearly not something unique to a schizophrenic person. This process operates in everyone to one degree or another.

Having discussed the concept of differentiation, its relationship to the degree of unresolved emotional attachment to the parental family may be more easily understood. *The degree to which a person functions as an undifferentiated self in their adult life reflects the degree to which they functioned as an undifferentiated self while growing-up in their family.* The mere fact of leaving one's parental family resolves nothing in terms of differentiation. Another way of saying this is that the more a person's growing-up years were governed by the emotional aspects of family relationships, the more they were functioning as an undifferentiated person in that family. They were, to whatever degree, programmed to have their thinking, feelings and behavior dictated by relationships. Everyone, including the person himself, played a role in this.

While everyone in a family is influenced by the emotional system to some degree, certain children are more influenced by it than others. The greater the intensity of the emotional process that surrounds a given child, the greater will be both the undifferentiation of that child and the child's eventual unresolved attachment to the family. People do not "differentiate" from their families in adolescence or when they leave home. What occurs at those times is varying degrees of cutting-off from the family emotional process and not a resolution of family emotional process. The freer a given child has been from the family problem, the less that child has had their development governed by the emotional aspects of relationships. Such a child has more energy available to develop as an individual and is freer to have an objective view of parents and siblings. These children are involved with the family, but can develop more of a direction for themselves that is not governed by the family's emotional reactivity and subjectivity. This "free spirit" grows up as a more differentiated person than the sibling or siblings who are more intensely caught up in the system. They will, therefore, have less of an unresolved emotional attachment to the family as adults. It is worth re-emphasis that what is being described is not an all-or-none process. These are gradations that exist between siblings.

The emotional process that *actually* existed in one's family is often different from what people *felt* it was. Some people who were intensely entangled in the emotional problem of their family feel they were not particularly involved in it at all. Such people often explain whatever problems they may encounter in their adult relationships on the basis of never having had close attachments while growing up. This viewpoint is often expressed in statements like the following: "My family was cold and did not express feelings. There was little affection. As a consequence, I need a great deal from others." This person is the product of a fairly intense attachment to family. They are replicating that attachment in adult relationships. When the adult relationships become too intense, they adopt the same distancing posture to deal with that intensity that they used as a child. In the process of distancing, they may lose their positive feelings for the other person, but this loss of feeling does not result from lack of involvement. It results from too much involvement.

As implied by what has already been discussed, the character of the unresolved emotional attachment different people have with their families can be quite variable. It can range from a highly conflictual relationship to an overly idealized, harmonious relationship. There can be just as much lack of resolution at either end of this spectrum. The undifferentiation in a relationship can have a positive or negative tone. *The critical component to be understood and observed is not the tone of the relationship, but how much the thinking, feelings and behavior of each person is regulated by the emotional forces in the relationship.* There is just as much undifferentiation in a relationship in which two people automatically move toward agreement to avoid a sense of separateness as there is in a relationship in which two people automatically disagree to avoid a sense of lack of separateness. Both postures are determined by the emotional reactivity of people and are a product of the lack of differentiation of self. As described earlier, there are people who adopt a pseudoindependent posture with their families. This is not differentiation. It is just pretending—not necessarily consciously—that one is not influenced by the family and does not need them.

The way people manage their lack of differentiation of self and unresolved emotional attachment to the past generations is described by a specific concept in systems theory called *emotional cut-off.* This concept describes the fact that the more intense the unresolved attachment or lack of differentiation, the greater the tendency for people to cut-off emotionally from each other in order to stabilize relationships and achieve comfort. Comfort achieved in this way is done at the price of emotional distance. People are not necessarily happy with this kind of "solution", but settle for it as a compromise. Emotional cut-off from one's family is not good or bad. Such judgments miss the point. It is simply the product of the emotional forces in a relationship system. A significant degree of cut-off, like the emotional forces that spawn it, is the product of *many generations* of evolving emotional process in a family. Blaming it on a person or even a few people is a very narrow perspective.

The lower the level of differentiation in a family system, the less that thinking and objectivity act as a counterbalancing force to emotional reactivity and subjectivity. As branches of the multigenerational family move toward greater levels of undifferentiation, the members of that family become increasingly torn between the need for a sense of connection with others and the fear of being taken-over, smothered, and impaired by relationship with others. It is a fact, regardless of our frequent wish to deny it, that a person's physical, emotional and social functioning is significantly influenced by family relationships. Emotional cut-off is a way of managing the intensity of these relationships and the forces that generate that cut-off must be recognized and respected. There is not a rule that says people "should" be in better emotional contact with their families. Each individual's situation is approached differently. It depends on a person's basic level of differentiation and the particular nature of the family system. Some families do not do well when people try to get more involved with each other. This is why a sound theoretical understanding of the family is so very important and why it is difficult to define more than general rules for dealing with one's family.

There are two basic types of emotional cut-off, although most cut-off is a mixture of both. The first type is physical distance. When people see each other less often and for briefer periods, the emotional intensity of the relationship inevitably subsides. This fact is not peculiar to the human, but is a characteristic of most organisms in nature. Physical distance can give the illusion of having worked something out in a relationship. Many people say they can visit their parental family and manage the visit adequately for a day or two. After that time, the emotional intensity begins to escalate and the old problems surface. The rising tensions might be manifested in over-drinking, depression, back pain, overt conflict or a variety of other things. It is an interesting paradox that family members can genuine-ly look forward to getting together, but once in the physical pres-ence of each other, tension increases and people seek distance. This tension is not by anyone's design, but is a product of how everyone is acting. It goes beyond the individuals involved. The emotional patterns that govern what happens in a family have come down through the generations. The play is similar to plays performed fifty and a hundred years ago. It is only the actors that have changed.

The second type of emotional cut-off is accomplished through an individual's internal mechanisms. A person can be physically pres-ent in the family, but emotionally distant or insulated in a variety of ways. People withdraw into television, books, fantasy, alcohol, drugs, preoccupation with health, depression, etc. The list is end-less. People also cut-off by avoiding discussion of emotionally charged issues. All of us have a tendency to want to avoid dealing with the potential reactions in the other person generated by dis-cussing emotional issues. We avoid in the name of protecting the other, but avoidance is really designed to protect ourselves. This statement is not to be taken to mean that people "should" bridge emotional cut-off by insisting feelings be expressed and emotional-ly-charged issues be discussed. It is never that simple.

Evaluating the degree of emotional cut-off is always difficult and there is a great deal still to be learned about it. The amount of geo-graphical distance between family members can be, but is not neces-sarily, an accurate indicator of cut-off. There are people in good emotional contact with their families despite living at great dis-tances. There are people who live physically close to their families who are quite emotionally insulated from them. There are people who move across country in the name of a better job opportunity, but who, in actuality, are trying to insulate themselves from their original families. It is not uncommon for one spouse to talk another spouse into doing this. Cut-off is not accurately measured by count-ing the number of communications between people in the form of letters and phone calls. So often these things become ritualized and provide the illusion of a closer connection than really exists. The only rule-of-thumb for assessing cut-off is that appearances are usually deceiving. Accurate evaluation is dependent on a good understanding of theory, particularly the concept of differentiation.

Emotional cut-off is not only an important concept to be understood theoretically, but it is also significant clinically because of the complications associated with it. The major complication is that the more people cut-off emotionally from family of origin, the greater the tendency to invest unrealistically in new relationships. This unrealistic investment contributes to the unresolved problems with the past generations being played out with the present and future generations. Some version of the old problem comes out in one's marriage and with one's children. Many people start their new families with a determination to correct what they perceived as their parent's mistakes. Implicit in this kind of attitude is a denial of one's own part in whatever problems existed. If a person perceived their father as distant, they themselves played a part in maintaining that distance. If they saw their mother as difficult to please, the person played out the opposite side of that problem. In general, when a person blames his parents, they will also blame others for problems in their future relationships. When a person idealizes their parents and puts most of the blame on themselves, the tendency is to repeat that pattern in future relationships. Problems repeat through the generations because the emotional forces that drive them are strong and it is difficult for people to be objective about themselves or the past. Determination alone to change things does not usually work because one's efforts rest on false assumptions about the nature of the problem.

In addition to increasing the tendency to replicate the problems of the past emotional cut-off is important clinically for another reason. Cut-off undermines the potential of the extended family system to operate as a support system for the nuclear family. In the absence of such viable connection with the extended network, many people substitute various kinds of social relationships. While these relationships are important, they generally do not have the potential of one's own family for being a durable and meaningful support system. There is something in the nature of familial bonds that is unique.

Given the theoretical assumption that every person has some degree of unresolved emotional attachment to the past generations and that this attachment is managed with varying degrees of emotional cut-off, the purpose in focusing on family of origin in therapy is to move toward some resolution of this attachment and to reduce cut-of. The primary obstacles to achieving this exists within the person making such an effort, although there are important obstacles within the family system as well. People do not achieve emotional separation from their families by staying away from them. Emotional separation is achieved while *in* relationship to important others. It is accomplished by staying in contact with the family and continually working toward emotional change within oneself. Focus on family of origin is often interpreted as an attempt to improve one's family relationships. Improving relationships is kind of a nebulous goal. It is the change within oneself, accomplished while in relationship to others, that permits relationships to improve. Statements such as, "My parents will never change," indicate the person has completely missed this point. Such a statement puts the focus on the other and not on self.

Another important reason for undertaking an effort like this with one's family is to develop the ability to think systems in reference to human behavior. The capacity for systems thinking depends on the ability to stay objective and to maintain a broad perspective. While people can generally do this when they are not emotionally involved in the subject at hand, they quickly lose that ability in emotional situations. There is something about the emotional arena of one's parental family that is ideal for working on the vulnerability of losing a systems perspective. Progress toward systems thinking in reference to one's family is dependent on a number of things. Most importantly it depends on the ability to contain one's emotional reactivity to the family more effectively and to get beyond making biased assessments of others. People sometimes claim to have gotten beyond these things with their families, but continue to be reactive and biased about the world around them. If somebody is really making progress in their family, that progress will be reflected in an improved capacity to see society as an emotional system all its own, and to relate to it on that basis. This is obviously not accomplished on the basis of a few trips back to see the family. There is so much to be learned and thought through that change occurs only gradually over a period of years.

The capacity to observe emotional systems and oneself in relationship to the system is, obviously, very important in all of this. Not everyone can do this. At least, not everyone can do it to the same degree. People usually begin with some minimal ability to view the family as a system and gradually improve that ability based on time and effort. There is a simplicity and complexity to emotional systems. They are simple in the sense that once you have sufficient detachment to be able to see the connectedness of people's thinking, feelings, emotional reactions and behavior, you can just sit back and watch the predictable sequences unfold. At the same time, with the broadening of one's observing lens, it is easier to appreciate the complexity of a system. The complexity is a product of all the variables that come into view that are important to be considered in understanding what is happening. Awareness of this complexity frees people from simplistic and narrow notions about why people do the things they do. It also frees people from equally simplistic notions about what it takes to "fix" problems.

When someone is caught in an emotional system, there is really no solution to the overall problem as long as the person remains in an emotionally reactive position. An emotionally reactive stance is characterized by such things as making compromises to get a little peace, doing things that shift the system's focus off oneself and onto someone else, or simply withdrawing and trying to avoid the problems. These actions and inactions often provide short-term relief for people, but the overall system problem remains unchanged. People play out the same scenarios day after day, month after month for years and nothing changes. Each time the scenario is played out, it is done in the name of making things better, correcting wrongs, "helping" someone, etc. In most respects, it is a mindless process that is driven by anxiety and emotional reactivity. Some resolution of the emotional problem of a relationship system can occur if at least one person can achieve just a little more detachment and neutrality than they have had in the past. This is never easy for anyone to achieve. Without that detachment, people are usually desperate for "answers" and typically look to the therapist to provide them. If a therapist suggests techniques to an emotionally reactive person who fails to appreciate the need for a new perspective on the problem, then that therapist has become part of the family problem. It amounts to the therapist trying to train someone to pretend to be different in their family and little *of long term value* is ever accomplished with such an approach. The key rests in people's capacity to view the problem just a little more objectively. If people can see that threats, wimpering, yelling, preaching, cajoling and avoiding are the very things that undermine people being individuals, then it becomes possible to work toward a different direction for oneself. Operating from a position of a little more perspective, the person is not using techniques designed to change others. The person is simply thinking more for themselves and exhibiting the courage to act on what they think. There are so many things in all of us that work against objectivity about our families. One of the biggest obstacles to gaining a different perspective is people's feeling that if they do not go on the way they have always done it, it amounts to giving up. They see no alternative to what has always "felt" right. Reacting emotionally even gets equated with "caring" and being "involved." Other obvious obstacles to thinking and acting more objectively are the guilt, the blaming of others, feeling sorry for others, self-righteousness, selfishness and the urge to reject people. When one person in a relationship system can get just a little beyond these kind of reactions, particularly when the anxiety in the system is high, the other people in the system will automatically sense it and benefit from it.

IMPORTANT MISCONCEPTIONS

Few subjects in the family therapy field have generated more interest than focus on the family of origin. Along with this interest, numerous misconceptions have also developed about the theory and approach to extended family. Given that systems theory, as applied to human behavior, is a new and radical departure from individual theory, misconceptions about it are probably unavoidable.

Family emotional systems theory is not something that can be learned in a classroom. Nor can it be adequately understood through extensive reading. While lectures and reading contribute something, *learning to think systems in relationship to human behavior is dependent on emotional changes occurring within the learner.* These emotional changes only occur gradually and as the result of considerable effort. As a consequence, learning systems theory is necessarily a gradual process. People may attend a workshop and pick up one or two superficial systems concepts rather quickly, but there is far more to systems theory than is learned in that way.

Defining the nature of emotional changes is difficult. The changes that must occur fall into two general areas. First, there is the requirement for a greater ability to distinguish between behavior that is based on the thinking process and behavior that is based on the feeling and emotional process. Second, there is the need for more ability to distinguish between subjectivity and objectivity. Subjectivity refers to the way the world is *perceived.* Objectivity refers to the way the world *is.* These two tasks are, obviously, not ones anyone ever completes. These are things that people with the motivation work at indefinitely. The misconceptions that arise about systems theory seem most often to occur when people attempt to bypass the changes just described. There are no shortcuts to learning to think in terms of emotional systems and differentiation.

A problem in discussing misconceptions is that many readers will assume that these are misconceptions held by others. We all have these misconceptions to some degree. There is a strong tendency in everybody to quickly assume that they understand systems theory and to treat it as a fixed and complete body of knowledge. Systems theory is only a beginning. It currently provides little more than a blueprint for the future. There is still so much to be understood.

The first misconception to be discussed is the confusion that exists about the concepts of emotional detachment and differentiation. Questions are continually asked about what it means to be in good contact with an emotional system and to still remain "outside" it. Some of the confusion about this idea stems from a misunderstanding about how systems theory conceptualizes emotions and feelings. This misunderstanding is reflected in frequently heard remarks such as, "Bowen's theory is anti-emotion. It advocates the suppression of emotion and feeling." In attempting to respond to this misperception, Bowen and others have used words like "contain" and "control" in reference to emotional reactivity, but these words have also been subject to considerable misinterpretation. A brief review of the basic assumptions about feelings and emotions made by systems theory might alleviate some of the confusion.

Systems theory views *homo sapiens* as a product of evolution and as governed by the same natural laws that govern all life on earth. This evolutionary heritage has endowed man with an emotional system, a system that, when disturbed, is believed to play an important role in the physical, emotional and social dysfunctions. Human beings, in other words, are not only descended from nature, but remain an integral part of nature. The terms *feeling* and *emotion* are not used synonymously in systems theory. Feelings are man's awareness of the more superficial aspects of the emotional system. They are a recent evolutionary acquisition. Emotions are phylogenetically much older and related closely to instincts. By defining emotion in this way, it is then accurate to say that birds, whales, mice and men are all governed by emotional reactions. In this respect, these animals are all very much alike. Man appears to be unique in nature in terms of his well-developed capacity to experience feelings. This capacity to experience feelings represents only a minor variation on the larger theme of the evolution of the emotional system, yet the human has tended to emphasize feelings over emotion in the understanding of human behavior. Throughout history, human beings have been so busy defining themselves as separate from nature that the task of defining commonalities with other living things has scarcely begun. We have ignored the obvious in the name of man being unique. We have done this in spite of having a wonderful evolutionary gift that permits *homo sapiens* to be the only form of life on earth able to observe the emotional system and to define the principles that govern it. This evolutionary gift is man's intellectual system.

The rapid and extensive evolutionary development of man's intellectual system has few parallels in nature. The "thinking brain" is indeed a natural wonder. Evolution did not grant the human an intellectual system that operates as a free agent. Its functioning, to a great extent, is governed by the emotional system and it operates in the service of the emotional system. To the extent that the intellectual system fails to operate as a free agent, it provides a subjective view of the real world—a view heavily colored by man's needs, wishes, and fears. It sees the world as the emotional system dictates it be seen and not as it is. There is nothing wrong with a subjective view of the world. Such a view presumably serves a function in human existence. It is important, however, to be able to recognize the difference between subjectivity and objectivity.

While much of the human intellectual system is governed by the emotional system, the intellect does have some capacity to operate free of emotional influence. Unencumbered by emotionality, the intellect can objectively observe one's inner emotional states and one's behavior. The intellectual system can observe, describe and develop concepts about human behavior that are firmly grounded in those observations. The concepts can be altered and even discarded as new observations come to light. The intellectual system "strives" to define the world as it is without what human subjectivity imposes on it.

Given the theoretical assumptions just outlined, it would be difficult to regard systems theory as anti-emotions. It is a theory about emotions. Saying it is anti-emotions is equivalent to saying it is against the behavior of whales, bats, man, fish, spiders and all the other wonderful creatures that inhabit this planet. The behavior of plants and animals is a fact of nature. Nobody is "against" such things. It is failure to appreciate this broad perspective of systems theory that generates so much confusion about this subject on a clinical level. People do repress and suppress feelings and deny the influence of their emotionality. There are certain clinical complications associated with doing these things. Other people are at the opposite end of the spectrum. They are constantly externalizing their feelings in almost obligatory fashion. Feelings are externalized in the name of not permitting a buildup of intolerable pressure. The higher the anxiety at any given moment, the greater the tendency for people to move toward one or the other of these extremes. In many marriages each partner plays out the opposite end of the spectrum and each feels intolerant and threatened by the way the other does it. A given level of differentiation can be characterized by either end of this dichotomy. Both partners in the marriage are equally emotionally reactive, but manage their emotionality and feelings in different ways. The lower the level of differentiation, the more intense the suppression and denial, or the more intense the obligatory expression of emotion and feeling. To regard one method of dealing with emotion as preferable to another is to lose a systems perspective.

Systems theory has defined an alternative to the suppression and obligatory expression of emotions and feelings. It is a method of managing emotionality and feelings that *depends on increased awareness and a gradual learning process.* This learning seems to occur at several levels. At the ''upper'' levels the learning involves the development of new ways of thinking about the emotional and feeling process within oneself and as it exists in the environment. At the ''deeper'' levels it seems to involve a kind of deprogramming of one's emotional reactivity, at least to some extent. People who use biofeedback to gain some control over a physiological system find it difficult to explain how they achieved that control. The learning involved in managing emotionality as described here is equally difficult to explain. Progress is definitely dependent on the intellectual system operating somewhat as a free agent. This permits a little more objectivity in one's observations, although observations alone are not enough. The individual must think about these observations and draw some conclusions. They must make up their minds about the nature of the emotional process and subjectivity that is part of them and around them and, based on that knowledge, pursue a constructive direction. This process is an important component of being more of a self. There is something about going through this process that tones down emotional reactivity and permits the person more options in emotionally charged situations. What is being described is not intellectualization. Intellectualization is a psychological defense mechanism whose activity is governed by emotional reactivity.

The emotional field of one's family of origin appears to be the ideal arena for working on the learning process that has just been outlined. Frequent contacts, coupled with the opportunity for periods of physical distance, with an emotional system to which one is vulnerable provide the opportunity for gaining objectivity about the system and about oneself in relationship to that system. Without contact, it is difficult for this kind of learning to occur. There is a lot more involved then simply going to visit relatives. Many people go through the motions of visiting family and learn nothing at all. Such people have great difficulty seeing the family as an emotional unit and their part in it, no matter how many visits they make. Role playing with non-family members in an attempt to recreate the past does not provide anywhere near the same opportunity that actual contact with family of origin provides.

Contacts with extended family, particularly during periods of high emotional intensity, cannot be done in a haphazard fashion. When some people make contact with an anxious system, they become so flooded with the prevailing emotionality that they just cannot think. They pull back from the family, literally to survive. Such occurrences do not necessarily mean that the person can never work on themselves in relationship to their original families. It just means the emotional forces that fuel the cut-off from their family are very intense and careful planning of their efforts is essential. When other people establish better contact with family, they are welcomed as long lost friends. There are problems associated with that kind of reception too. These kind of differences in people and families are part of the reason an objective ''coach'' is required to assist people with their parental families. People are never calm enough and objective enough when they begin such a project to not need a way of monitoring when they are getting lost.

If people begin with at least a thread of objectivity about the emotional process in their families, and have the motivation to continue their efforts over a long period of time, they can gradually achieve more ability to be in contact with the system while retaining some level of detachment and neutrality. This means being neutral and not pretending to be neutral. Neutrality is reflected more in actions than words. Proclamations such as, ''I'm not taking sides,'' mean little to a family and accomplish less. The concept of emotional detachment with one's family is sometimes interpreted as being uninvolved or even as being selfish. The opposite is actually the case. A little better level of differentiation of self and its accompanying neutrality is dependent on being more aware of the emotional currents in the system than in the past. It is a process of reducing the degree of emotional cut-off from important people. Emotional cut-off is a product of people's emotional reactiveness and the distorted images people hold about one another. The capacity to have one's behavior less directed by one's emotional reactivity and skewed notions about others, and less directed by the emotional reactivity and biases of others about you, permits closer and more sustained contact. When people say things like, "My family won't let me grow up" or "I've outgrown my family," they are talking from an emotionally reactive and biased position. They are seeing the problem as in the family and not in themselves.

A second prevalent misconception, closely related to what has just been described, involves the concept of togetherness. Family systems theory is frequently perceived as anti-togetherness. Togetherness is "supposed" to be a good thing that everyone strives to achieve. If that is the case, why does systems theory put such emphasis on individuality? In the confusion, individuality itself even gets defined as "anti-togetherness." To get stuck on either end of this individuality-togetherness dichotomy is to lose a systems perspective. Systems theory encompasses *both* individuality and togetherness. Systems theory defines togetherness as a life force that inclines people toward maintaining a sense of emotional connection with each other. The togetherness force also triggers actions in response to real or imagined threats to that connection. There is a counterbalancing life force called individuality that inclines people to be emotionally separate and autonomous beings. Both these life forces are essential to human existence. The capacity to sustain emotional closeness as well as the ability to tolerate periods of emotional distance are a product of both the individuality and togetherness forces. When people have a limited capacity to be individuals, they are vulnerable to the emotional interplay of relationships. They can easily feel smothered or abandoned in a relationship and overreact to the emotional needs of others. These feelings and reactions are a product of the togetherness force not being sufficiently balanced by individuality. One's functioning is at the mercy of the environment. The greater the degree of undifferentiation, the more this is the case. It sounds like a paradox, but the felt lack of togetherness is a product of too much togetherness. Considering systems theory as anti-togetherness results from the failure to perceive this basic interplay of the emotional forces in a system.

A third misconception about family of origin is that it means trying to be a therapist for one's family. Attempting to be a therapist for one's family is probably the major cause for failures in family of origin. Being a therapist carries the implication that one is trying to influence or change the family. It also carries the more subtle implication that one has the capacity to enlighten the family about "their" problem. This sort of an attitude fails to respect the family and fails to take into account one's own part in whatever problems exist. Confronting one's parents about how you perceive them to have misunderstood or mistreated you, or even feeling you are going to forgive your parents, are part of this omnipotent attitude. Others go home with a goal of getting everybody's feelings expressed and finally getting everybody together through "improved" communication. Nine times out of ten this kind of an effort blows up in people's faces. On occasion, if the family is not too anxious to start with, it can make things a little more harmonious, but the results are short-lived. These kinds of things have nothing to do with differentiation of self. This is not to say that an effort toward differentiation of a self in one's family of origin cannot have a favorable impact on the family. In fact, the long-term favorable impact on the family is probably the best measure of the effectiveness of one's efforts to be more of a self. If one person can be present and accounted for in his family and at the same time maintain a calm, clear and non-antagonistic stance, they will have a remarkably favorable influence on the system. This is an influence that occurs by virtue of who the person is, their attitudes and reactions, and not as a product of trying to change others.

The last misconception to be mentioned has been touched on briefly already and is probably the most pervasive. It is interpreting Bowen's focus on family of origin as nothing more than a therapeutic technique. In regarding it as simply a technique, the theoretical base that permits the approach in the first place is completely missed. This misperception is commonly expressed in statements such as, "I use the Bowen approach for certain cases." A therapist who makes such statements is usually constructing a family diagram and encouraging people to write and visit relatives. The nature of emotional systems as they evolve through the generations and the forces that create emotional cut-off have not been understood. The therapist talks "systems," but is still using individual psychodynamics to understand the family. If the therapist chooses to use individual psychodynamics to understand families, that is their choice. But calling such an approach "systems" is inaccurate and tends to obfuscate an important new theoretical understanding of human behavior.

TECHNIQUE

Before discussing the technical approach to family of origin, it is important to note that there is more to the task of differentiating a self than can be accomplished in relationship to one's family. While the family is very important, it is only a beginning. Some mastery over the emotional factors that undermine one's ability to be an individual in the family permits a better appreciation of how much that same emotional process occurs in areas unrelated to the family. We live in a largely subjective world, particularly in relationship to human behavior. Daily bombardments by the media, literature, the arts, social relationships and even the schools are often heavily laced with unspecified assumptions about what the world is like. Our thinking is influenced by these sources of subjectivity more than we realize. All of us are fairly vulnerable to this emotionally determined "group think." A serious effort toward differentiation necessitates thinking through these societal issues as objectively as possible and then having the courage to stand firm on one's beliefs. This effort to be more of a self in face of the social pressures that surround us is too complex a subject to be discussed in detail here. It is mentioned only as a reminder not to equate being more of a self in one's family with differentiation.

There are two factors that supersede all others in determining the effectiveness of whatever technical approach is taken in the family of origin. Both factors pertain to the person making the effort. The first factor is the individual's capacity to think theoretically about the family and to act on that basis. The actual techniques used are far less important than the continual effort to be aware of how one is thinking about the family and its problems. All of us adhere to many subjectively based assumptions about our families and behave on the basis of those assumptions. These assumptions are not changed by implementing a series of techniques. Using techniques without examining assumptions amounts to pretending to be different. When people change what they do on the basis of new ways of thinking, they are not pretending. Changes implemented on this basis are not really even techniques. People are just being themselves.

The second critical factor influencing one's effectiveness in family of origin is motivation. People must decide if they want to be present and accounted for in their families or if they want to continue to preserve a distance. Many people go through the motions of seeing more of their families without adequately addressing the issue of how important it is to them. They go through the motions on the basis of somebody suggesting it as a good idea. The question comes down to whether the people in the parental family are important enough to want more of a relationship with them. The project to be more of a self in one's family of origin is not a small undertaking. It has to be approached responsibly and not as a hit-and-run affair. There is more to the task than having some kind of "roots" experience or building an emotional support system. The support system aspect is of value, but there is more to differentiation of self than that. For this reason, a therapist does not "send people back to their families." The people themselves must first decide on the importance of doing it.

The attitude with which one approaches the family is also very important. No matter how much a person thinks he knows about his family and the people who comprise it, it must be approached with an attitude of having much to learn. It cannot be restated enough that much of one's attitudes and ways of behaving toward various family members are governed by subjectivity and emotional reactivity. To varying degrees, family members have related to one another on the basis of an emotionally driven group process, and not on the basis of each being individuals. When people can be a little more objective, think with a broader perspective, and relate as individuals, it is amazing how much more there is for people to learn about each other. People can live in the same household for years and know little about each other. Their emotional reactions to each other can tie them together in complex ways, but at the same time prevent them from being aware of each other's hopes, fears, goals, etc.

There are some general guidelines for the approach to extended family that can be defined. As mentioned earlier, it is difficult to be specific because of the wide variation in people and their situations. It is often easier to know what will not work rather than what will work for a given family. This is part of the reason that a person making an effort with his family always benefits from the help of a relatively objective "coach" or therapist who has accomplished a reasonable amount in relationship to his own family.

Some people begin their efforts having been quite distant from their families and having seen less and less of them in recent years. Such people usually readily admit that they hardly know their families, especially anybody other than their parents and siblings. Other people live in the midst of their family of origin and frequently say, "I do not see how I could know them any better than I do." There are people who are quite unrealistically emotionally dependent on their families, as well as those who do not depend on their families or permit their families to depend on them at all. There are all gradations between these extremes. Some families have gradually drifted apart over the years, while others have been blown apart by high levels of emotional intensity. How one is received by the family will be contingent, obviously, on the kind of situation that has prevailed. There are overtly harmonious, peace-agree families that tend to obliterate differences and highly conflictual families that exaggerate differences. It is impossible to detail all the variations in approach that are dictated by these variations in the character of families, but recognition of these variations underlines the fact that what has been effective in one family may not be useful in another. People may set out with the best of intentions to be in better contact with their families only to find their efforts thwarted by one obstacle after another. It is a sound theoretical understanding that permits one to make sense out of these obstacles and provide alternative routes of approach.

In most instances, working toward differentiation in family of origin depends on people being in more contact with the family than they have been in the past, and on being in contact with more members of the family. People frequently have a narrow view of what comprises their original family. They confine it to parents, siblings, and perhaps a few others and ignore the larger extended system. Frequent, relatively brief contacts with family generally contribute more to developing objectivity than infrequent, long visits. The ideal situation for working on differentiation is living close enough to the extended family to permit getting home frequently, but not so close that one cannot get sufficiently away from it to allow thinking through the experiences.

What has just been described is not to be taken as a "rule" for success in one's efforts. Motivated people can accomplish a great deal with far less than the ideal situation. The most productive visits are the ones when the individual goes alone. One does not take his spouse or other relative along for comfort and reinforcement if differentiation is the goal. Some people have interpreted this as meaning one "never" takes his spouse and children along. It is just that one has to make some of the visits on one's own. Again, in most instances, the overall thrust of one's effort with the family is to be more a part of things. The purpose is to put more life into various relationships and to reactivate an emotional process that has likely

grown dormant over the years. Certain people recoil at the suggestion of reactivating relationships and say things like, "If I get that
involved with my family, I will wind up feeling I am responsible for
their emotional well-being. It will be the same old story." Others
make comments like, "If I get too involved, I will fall back into the
child position." The fact that these things can happen when a person
gets more involved is precisely the reason for doing it. What happens is a function of the lack of resolution in the attachments. The
goal is to reactivate the process carefully so that it can be viewed
more objectively and worked on. The importance of being in better
contact with the emotional process in one's family makes it particularly important to go home at times when family anxiety is high.
Times of serious illness, funerals, marriages, anniversaries and
other such occasions are important times to be at home. If a person
has been a fairly cut-off person and not counted on to be present at
these important times in the past, there is no point in getting mad at
the family for being treated as a cut-off person. Cut-off is a two-
sided process. In making these trips, it is important to keep in mind
that a person is imprisoned by his idealizations of certain family
members and devaluation of other members. People are prisoners of
all the stories they have heard down through the years and of the
often distorted significance that the family has placed on certain
events. *It is the family emotional process that exaggerates and distorts events.* This emotional process is always more important for
directing the course of the family than whatever events might have
occurred. People, however, tend to blame events for what happens
and ignore the way people related around those events. It is this
emotionally driven relationship process that creates the "saints"
and "devils" in one's family and it is that process one is trying to
observe and understand.

Simply being in more contact with one's family does not automatically permit a person to see ordered relationship patterns in the
midst of sometimes quite chaotic situations. An understanding of the
concept of a triangle is what can bring some order to one's thinking
about the family. Triangles basically describe an important way in
which people manage the intensity of emotional attachments. In any
three person system in which people have some emotional significance to each other, two people will be relatively more involved
with one another and the third person will be an outsider. The involvement of the twosome can have either a positive or a negative
emotional tone. The degree to which the third person is excluded

can vary. Each of the three people plays an equal part in fostering the positions they occupy. Triangles are not static because people are constantly making moves to achieve a more comfortable position for themselves in the system. The greater the anxiety in the system, the more these various moves are in evidence. If the emotional intensity between the insiders reaches a level that their relationship becomes unstable, the outside position is more favorable. At these intense times, one of the insiders may try to pull the outsider into the situation. At other times, the cozy appearance of the relationship between the insiders may leave the outsider feeling painfully excluded. At such points, the outsider may make moves designed to break into the togetherness of the twosome.

One particularly important aspect of triangles is that the people who comprise them take sides on the various relationship issues that arise. If there is a conflict between the insiders, the outsider may become a new insider by being sympathetic with one side. When anxiety is low in the system, the patterns of the triangles may be barely visible. As anxiety increases, the various triangles become more active and are more easily observed. The more the undifferentiation in a system, the more chronic anxiety it generates, and the more chronically in evidence are the triangles. Triangles are important to understand because the concept helps place every family relationship in the context of all the other relationships. In other words, the emotional aspects of any family relationship, cannot be adequately understood out of context. Triangles are interlocking in that anxiety from one triangle can spill over into another triangle. For example, anxiety that first emerges in the relationship between two siblings may eventually get played out via a series of interlocking triangles in the relationship between the parents.

In a family consisting of a mother, father, son, and daughter there are four triangles: mother, father, and son; mother, father, and daughter; mother, son, and daughter; and father, son and daughter. One or two of these triangles are usually chronically more intense than the others. The most intense triangle is the one characterized by the least amount of differentiation in the relationships. The two parents, for example, may function with less differentiation in relationship to the son than they do in relationship to the daughter. This does not mean that on any given day a particular triangle is always the most intense. The process will shift around from day to day, but, on the average, certain triangles chronically lack more differentiation than others.

It is possible for a person to be relating actively in a triangle and to work gradually toward being more emotionally neutral about what goes on in the triangle. As described earlier, achieving more neutrality depends on becoming a more objective observer of the relationships and one's own part in those relationships. As also mentioned previously, being neutral and pretending to be neutral are two very different things. The pretense of neutrality is evident in proclamations such as, "I will not take sides," and, "I will not listen to any more of your stories about Dad." Another pretense of neutrality is making a rule about not keeping any family secrets. People usually make such statements and rules in an effort to extricate themselves from triangles. These things are ineffective when the person is still emotionally reactive and participating in the very thing they are claiming to be neutral about. Participants in a triangle easily recognize lack of neutrality, regardless of statements to the contrary. Where a person is genuinely neutral, whatever statements they make and actions they take do not polarize and antagonize the system. When a person is neutral, light-hearted, remarks have a calming effect on the system and are not perceived as "cold" or "sarcastic". To the extent that one's functioning in a system is governed by triangles, one is not being a self.

Considerable emphasis has been placed thus far on being less emotionally reactive to the family system. There is more to an effort toward differentiation than being less reactive, but it is a very important component. People can be fairly reasonable about most things when the system is calm. In a calm system people are more tolerant of differences and have an easier time permitting one another to be themselves. There are times, however, when the position or direction a person chooses to take stirs unavoidable emotional reactivity in the family. In these situations, the system will not calm down until it is very clear that the position one is taking will not be altered under the family's emotional pressure to give it up. It is at these times that a person making an effort to be more of a self stands most alone. The pressure from the system to blend back into the old togetherness is intense, and the pressure coming from within oneself to do that is also intense. The threat to oneself and to the system that is reacted to in these situations is the move toward more emotional separateness. Given that the long-term benefit to a system of one person being more of an individual is significant, it is interesting that the short-term backlash against it can be so intense. Such is the nature of emotional systems. Arriving at such positions in relationship to one's family is usually a complex process.

It is not easy to sort out the difference between an emotionally determined rebellion against the system and a more thoughtful direction for self. The system usually reacts the same way to both things. A thoughtful position is taken fairly calmly, respects the position of others, and is not designed to threaten or change others. It is not dictated by one's own anxiety. It is generally not indicated to take positions when the system is very anxious. Even a reasonably well thought-out position can flame the fires of a real anxious family. Many people try to take a position in their families and find themselves out on one end of a polarized debate in the family. This is not differentiation and accomplishes little for oneself or for the family. Thoughtful positions transcend the polarities.

The triangles in one's family are important, but they are not all equally important in terms of being fruitful arenas to work on differentiation of self. The triangles that involve one's mother are usually the most critical ones. This is the case because the relationship with one's mother has usually been the most emotionally intense. For most people, the relationship with their mother is the one in which their emotional vulnerability is the greatest. The fact that this relationship is intense is a product of many factors that operate in the family as a whole. Blaming this intensity on the mother completely misses the point. Regardless of how it comes to be the case, however, the emotional makeup of one's mother and her values are an extremely important influence on the development of one's own differentiation.

In a majority of instances, the triangle that involves oneself and one's parents is the most important in defining a self. Failing to recognize that the relationship one has with each parent is significantly governed by the operation of this triangle is a frequent stumbling block people encounter in working on their families. For example, people may set out to improve their relationship with a father whom they perceive to be "distant." They try and try and nothing much happens. What is missed is that the character of the relationship with one's father is influenced both by the character of the relationship with one's mother and the nature of the parents' relationship with each other. It is a triangle and in a triangle one does not pursue individual relationships and expect results. The goal is to achieve emotional neutrality in regards to the relationship between the two parents. If that can be achieved, a different kind of relationship with each parent *then* becomes possible. This is not a very easy thing to accomplish, however. Something more is required than just saying, "I no longer take sides in my parents' disputes." People grow up very entangled in the relationship with their parents. One cannot go home and just will themselves to be more objective about them. People are too close to the process. Some progress can be made in this way, but the intensity of the process undermines one's efforts. There are other reasons for not focusing exclusively on the parental triangle. The parental triangle does not exist in isolation. It is influenced by the interlocking triangles of the larger system. It is also a product of emotional forces passed down through the generations. It is necessary, therefore, to work toward placing the parental triangle in this larger perspective before a person can achieve much objectivity. Whatever resolution that occurs in the parental triangle, in other words, is heavily dependent on what one can accomplish in parts of the system a little more removed from one's immediate growing-up experience.

Triangles that involve oneself, a sibling, and one's mother can be quite important, but, again, can be difficult to become more objective about. The relationships with one's siblings are heavily influenced by the character of the relationship each sibling has with the parents. One can face the same obstacles in trying to improve a relationship with a sibling as those discussed earlier in reference to improving the relationship with one's father. The fact that these relationships are significantly governed by triangles cannot be forgotten. In general, it is quite difficult to accomplish anything in a sibling relationship until more differentiation has been achieved in relationship to one's parents. Remember that one grows up in these triangles and they are not resolved when a person leaves home. They frequently grow dormant when people become adults and are on their own, but the basic circuits of the triangle are still in place and can be reactivated. Even if one's parents have died, the sibling relationships can still be governed by the old triangles. One example of a sibling triangle is the following. While growing up, a person's attitude and way of reacting emotionally to a particular sibling was strongly influenced by having taken sides in the interaction between the mother and that sibling. The person was vulnerable to the mother's anxiety and feelings toward that sibling and the person blamed the sibling for the distress the mother experienced. In other words, this person functioned in the relationship with that sibling as an extension of his mother. The sibling, in turn, related to the person as an extension of his mother. Each member of the triangle contributed equally to this process and it was also reinforced by the other interlocking triangles in the family. If the person attempts to be more of a self in this triangle, usually the most difficult aspect of the effort is overcoming one's vulnerability to mother's anxiety and point of view. If a person can become more objective about that process with the parent, it is surprising how rapidly feelings toward the sibling can resolve. Again, this does not mean that the mother is to blame for the patterns in these triangles. She is just one participant in a mutually reinforcing process.

The most profitable triangles in which to work on being more objective about the family process are those that exist in the previous generations. Objectivity gained in these triangles which have been somewhat removed from immediate experience can contribute significantly to objectivity about the triangles that involve one's siblings and parents. It is a littler easier to be objective about things from which one has been slightly removed. Objectivity about the past can carry over into more immediate situations because the present is, in many respects, a replay of the past. The basic goal of focusing on the previous generations' triangles is to begin to view one's parents from the perspective of their relationships with their families of origin. One's mother is the daughter of one's grandparents. When a person begins to try and understand his parents in this way, it is amazing how quickly he can become more detached. While growing up, most people are so caught up in their direct experiences with their parents that they could not think about their parents in any other context.

An example of working on oneself in the context of a triangle that belongs to the past generations is the following. Your mother was the younger of two sisters. Her father died about the time your parents were married, but your early childhood years included fairly frequent visits to see your aunt and grandmother. There was always a certain amount of conflict between mother and her sister, but it never exceeded a manageable level. When you were a young teenager, your grandmother died and the circumstances surrounding her funeral exacerbated the tensions between your mother and your aunt to the point that they would no longer see each other. You grew up feeling your aunt was basically to blame for the problems, a viewpoint supported by both your parents. The basic problem that led to the cut-off between the sisters was not the events or particular actions that people tend to implicate. *It relates to the old unresolved triangle between your grandmother, your aunt, and your mother.* When you cut-off from your aunt too, you have become part of the undifferentiation that perpetuates the interlocking triangles. It is constructive for you to "bridge" the cut-off with your aunt. It is constructive if your goal is a better level of differentiation of self. It can contribute something not only to you, but to the family as a whole. In the first place, making contact with your aunt gives you the opportunity to see both sides of the relationship problem between your mother and aunt. In the second place, it can confront you with your vulnerability to your mother's emotional reactions to your making the contact. Working on that vulnerability within oneself is an essential ingredient of working on differentiation. One is not doing this to oppose one's mother, even though it may be perceived that way. Taking this kind of action communicates more to the family about being a self than any amount of talking about being a self. As mentioned earlier, from an emotional standpoint, it is a littler easier to do this kind of thing in a triangle that involves the past generation. The objectivity and abilities gained in the past generations' triangles, however, will contribute to one's abilities to accomplish similar things in the parental and sibling triangles. There are, obviously many variations in the past generations' triangles from that just described.

Another major component of the effort toward differentiation of self in family of origin is a multigenerational study of one's family. Such a study encompasses much more than basic genealogy. The basic purpose of the research is to enable a person to think about the emotional process in the family in multigenerational terms. The family is an emotional system that evolves down through the generations in fairly predictable ways. There is a basic emotional connectedness between the generations that results in each generation having a significant influence on the emotional process in the generations that follow. There are people who reject such an idea, believing it to be too "fatalistic" a view of the human process. Rejection of the idea of a basic emotional connectedness between the generations is reflected in statements such as, "I am different from my parents and I intend to raise my children differently than I was raised." Used in this context, the word different usually implies better. Many of the changes people make to establish themselves as different from their parental families are superficial changes. They create the illusion of change when, in fact, the basic underlying emotional process from the past has undergone little modification. The greater the denial of the influence of the past, the greater the tendency to replicate the past. Revolting against one's past, in other words, is a process that prevents change. Some change can emerge from an objective assessment of the past and its influence on oneself. One of the real values of doing a multigenerational history is that people can then make up their own minds about how the emotional process of the past is being reflected in the present. One need not take anybody else's word for this. When five or six generations of a family are carefully studied, fairly wide variations in the functioning of nuclear family units and individuals are always observable. It is not the nature of families to maintain a status quo. Certain lines of family will show gradual improvement in functioning and other lines will show gradual deterioration. Sometimes fairly significant shifts occur within just three or four generations, although the process is usually a gradual one. The fact that these changes occur is irrefutable. Systems theory proposes that these changes bear an important relationship to the evolving multigenerational emotional process in a family.

Developing a history of the emotional process in one's family is based on a wedding between theoretical understanding and information about the family gleaned from many sources. The best resources are the family members themselves, although the various written resources that are readily available contribute a great deal as well. Information such as birth dates, death dates, causes of death, occupations, education, health history, divorce data, where people lived, and the variety of stories one hears about people can all help bring the emotional process of the past generations back to life. Just getting to know some of the more distant relatives a little better can give a person a better sense of the larger family and what it is like. The theoretical concepts can be used to help organize all this information. For example, systems theory defines three basic ways that the undifferentiation of a nuclear family can be expressed. It can be expressed in marital conflict, dysfunction in a spouse, and dysfunction in one or more children. A nuclear family unit that lived a hundred and fifty years ago had these same "options" available to it. Since one approaches the family with these basic hypotheses about the way families function, it does not take a lot of data to allow one to define the emotional process that existed four or five generations in the past. When a person begins to see his family as a series of interlocking emotional fields extending back through the generations, thinking about why people do the things they do takes on new meaning. Who does one blame for the fact that things evolved the way they did? This is, obviously, a rhetorical question.

There are a number of special situations related to family of origin that occur frequently enough to merit comment. One such situation is when one or both parents are dead. Death of a parent does not preclude resolving something that existed in the relationship with that parent. The approach for doing this is to make contact with people who were an important part of the emotional field that surrounded the parent. The dead parent's living siblings, uncles, aunts, cousins, and even very close friends can all contribute something to one's efforts. In making better emotional contact with these people, it is generally not useful to approach them with comments like, "Tell me about my father." Useful information and insights come gradually and are a product of the relationships developed with people. When somebody assaults the family with a barrage of questions, the answers that result are often of dubious value. If one approaches these people with patience and an open mind, in time a more objective picture of one's parent can emerge. The most valuable people with whom to develop relationships are those for whom your dead parent had emotional significance and who themselves were fairly important to the overall functioning of the family.

There are a few people who say they have no family. Everyone is dead. In most such circumstances there are people somewhere. There may only be a few first or second cousins, but such people can frequently make an important contribution to one's effort to make emotional contact with the past and to develop a broader perspective. Highly motivated people can often accomplish a great deal with only limited family resources.

In the majority of instances, when a person has been adopted, their adoptive family is the emotional system that contributes the most to an effort toward differentiation. This is almost always the case when the person has been adopted very early in life. When people have been adopted a little later in their lives, then the biological family does have more emotional significance and is valuable to explore. There are people who were adopted as infants, but make a great deal out of the fact that they are adopted. They often have an intense emotional urge to contact their biological family. The basic emotional problem in such cases is the undifferentiation that exists between the person and the *adoptive* family. The preoccupation with the biological family represents an emotional cut-off from the adoptive family. This is a problem that is not solved through contact with the biological family, but has to be resolved in relationship to the adoptive family.

When differentiation of self in family of origin became better known, many mental health professionals questioned its significance as a form of psychotherapy. Many regarded learning more about one's family as an interesting exercise, but not as something useful in producing "deep psychic" changes. *A reasonably successful effort at differentiation of self in family of origin has the potential for producing changes within the individual that extend beyond what can be accomplished with other forms of psychotherapy.* This is not something that can be easily explained. Certainly the sense of having more of a connection to one's family and the past is important to people. It has a calming effect. An emotional connection by itself, however, does not necessarily resolve one's feelings about parents and the larger family. Unresolved feelings about the past are a product of subjectivity and other aspects of one's undifferentiation. People can ventilate these feelings to a therapist or a friend, but that process contributes little to their resolution. Ventilation provides only temporary relief. *Feelings do resolve based on a more objective view of oneself and of the family.* In addition, a person's level of chronic anxiety can be reduced by achieving a little better level of basic differentiation of self. This reduction in chronic anxiety seems to result from gaining the confidence that one can retain a self even in very intense emotional environments. There is something about such confidence that relaxes people. This does not mean that it is necessary for people to work constantly at differentiation in their important relationship systems. It only means that they know they can call on it when it is important to have it.

REFERENCE

Anonymous. Toward the differentiation of a self in one's own family. In: J. Framo (Ed.), *Family Interaction.* New York: Springer, 1972.

Family of Origin as a Training Resource for Family Therapists

Shirley Braverman

People develop their sense of self and their interpersonal skills in their families of origin. Omitting any focus on the family of origin in training removes a tremendously useful learning resource. The dilemma for the teacher is to find the boundary between teaching and therapy. The author describes her approach and suggests how it can be kept within a teaching framework, be case related and unintrusive.

The balance between didactic teaching, supervision of case material and experiential learning in the training of family therapists has long been a problem in the field. Since there was very little theory, the first generation of family therapists was trained by supervision of case material. Later, some psychodynamic and systems theory was added to the training. The growth therapists added an emphasis on experiential learning, with the result that the use of simulated families emerged. It was used as a technique for teaching therapists interviewing skills and, when they role-played family members, to help them experience what it felt like to be in a certain kind of family. An extension of the growth therapists' interest in experiential learning has been their focus on the family of origin as a resource in training. Those training programs which consider psychodynamic understanding important tend to emphasize the personal developmental experience of the therapist as an important aspect of his/her training. The dilemma for the teacher in doing family

Shirley Braverman, M.S.W., is Associate Professor, McGill School of Social Work, Family Therapy Training Program, Institute of Community and Family Psychiatry, Jewish General Hospital, Montreal, Quebec.

Address reprint requests to: Shirley Braverman, Institute of Community and Family Psychiatry, Jewish General Hospital, 4333 Cote Ste. Catherine Road, Montreal, Quebec H3T 1E2.

Reprinted by permission from *Candian Journal of Psychiatry,* Volume 27, No. 8, December 1982, pp. 629-633.

of origin work as part of a training program is to find the boundary between teaching and therapy. After 20 years of supervising and teaching family therapy the author is just beginning to find that boundary. This paper is an attempt to share that experience and to open the subject for further discussion and study.

IMPORTANCE OF FAMILY OF ORIGIN WORK

Since people develop their sense of self and their interpersonal skills in their families of origin, omitting any focus on the family of origin in training removes a tremendously useful learning resource. Framo[1] states that "when we train students formally we continue the training they got from their parents, brothers, sisters, grandparents, aunts and uncles." Those family therapists who emphasize personal growth rather than a more specific problem-solving approach consider self knowledge and family of origin experience to be extremely important for the therapist. Napier and Whitaker[2] have stated that "perhaps the most serious problem in family therapy, the therapist's transference, can also be a powerful stimulus to his personal growth." Just as the client's experience in his family of origin will influence his present behaviour and relationships, so too can the therapist's family of origin experience be both helpful and a stumbling block in his task of learning to become a family therapist.

Robin and Prudence Skynner[3] have incorporated some family of origin work in their training program in England. The techniques they have used are family sculpting and the genogram. One person sculpts his family of origin and another person makes a genogram of his family.

Some teachers, like Virginia Satir, use family reconstructions which are three generational simulations of certain moments in the trainee's family of origin's life, as an experience in personal growth. It is intended to have an indirect effect on the trainee's capacity as a family therapist. Others like Framo[1], Ferber[4], Whitaker and Napier[2] are among those who have included some family of origin work in their training of family therapists.

CASE FOCUSED APPROACH

My own approach with students is more case focused than that of the growth therapists. It grew out of my experience as supervisor in the three year Family Therapy Training Program at the Institute of

Community and Family Psychiatry of the Jewish General Hospital in Montreal and as teacher of family therapy in the McGill University diploma course in Psychiatry.

The three year training program is open to professionals in various mental health disciplines. It consists mainly of social workers and psychologists but there have been a sprinkling of general practitioners, guidance counsellors, nurses and ministers. They come from a variety of institutions and meet once a week for 3 hours. Of this time, 1-1/2 hours is didactic teaching and watching a continuous case for part of the year and 1-1/2 hours is supervision in small groups for the entire year.

My experience with family of origin work started in this program. Because the students were working with real families we could not afford the luxury of a family of origin focus purely for the therapist's personal growth, however valid that might be. It had to grow out of a problem the student was having that did not disappear with cognitive understanding of the dynamics of the system, nor with the supervisor's suggestions for using different techniques to stimulate change. It was in an attempt to address that problem in training that I began to look to the family of origin as a resource.

DEVELOPMENT OF TRUST ESSENTIAL

There are two conditions that must be met before one starts family of origin work. One is that the student group must have developed a certain level of trust in each other and the supervisor and two, that cognitive understanding and technical suggestions have not helped the student overcome the problem. Development of trust is mandatory, otherwise the student experiences the process as an intrusion into his life and an attack on his competence as a person. Needless to say, no focus on the personal life of the student is begun without his/her wish to do so. A comment from the supervisor is made to the effect that there seems to be something else that is blocking him* in this particular case and it might be useful to go back to his family of origin experience to find out what it is. Does he wish to try? If the student says he would rather not, one should leave it and if the student is in individual therapy one then suggests he discuss it there. If he is not in individual therapy it is treated in the

---

*I shall continue to refer to the student as he, for purposes of brevity and to the supervisor or teacher as she, for the purpose of this article.

usual academic way, that is if the problem is not crippling enough for the student to fail the year it is ignored; if it is serious, the student is not permitted to continue his training because his performance as therapist has not met the required standard. The rationale for this approach is that people have different rates and styles of learning and as long as clients are not being harmed I would prefer to give the student time to master his problem in his own way.

PROCESS OF FAMILY OF ORIGIN WORK

If the student does wish to try, it is useful to have him start with a genogram so that the group and supervisor see his family constellation at once. The genogram is a family map which consists of the constellation of the family in which he grew up and the family of origin of each of his parents. The family of procreation is included if there is one. The student is only asked to describe the people and relationships in his family of origin and that of his parents. He is not asked about the relationships in his family of procreation because that is not the cause of his difficulty with his clients and also because that would be unnecessarily intrusive. One can take some distance in discussing one's family of origin. It is much more difficult to do so with one's family of procreation.

The student is then asked to draw a thick line between himself and the person or people he is closest to in the family and a wavy line between himself and the person or people with whom he has the most difficulty. He is asked to describe those relationships in greater detail so that the emotional flavour will clearly emerge. Often he will bring up memories of important incidents during this process. The affect, although present, does not tend to get too intense because there is not enough time for this to build up in a 1-1/2–2 hour session. Because the time is limited the student has more cognitive control than he has in an all day or week-end session devoted to an exploration of the family of origin. While less therapeutic, perhaps, the essential didactic purpose of the work is maintained.

After all the lines have been drawn and the descriptions given, we then look at whether there is any similarity between the people towards whom he had connected himself with a wavy or a thick line and any members of the client family. It does not take long for the pattern to emerge. The student tends to see the family member who reminds him most of a conflictual relative as sicker than he is: he does not see that person's strengths as clearly as he might see those of others, nor can he recognize certain behaviour as defensive and get to the underlying fear, as he has been able to do with other family members. Conversely, he tends to have some blind spots for those clients who are similar to an idealized relative. He will tend to have difficulty seeing how that person can be manipulative and destructive in the family. It is therefore important to go into the most positive relationships in the client family as well and link it to the student's idealized relationship in his family of origin. How do they begin to see their parents** in three dimensions? The process of understanding the client family and the student's difficulty starts with a description of the family of origin and moves to focus on the client family. Once the student can see intellectually what aspects of the individual client he has been denying, he is then asked to go back to the genogram to see whether he has any new ideas about the people to whom he was connected by wavy and strong lines. Usually the student begins at that point to see that they are not as black and white as he thought and that the similarities are striking. We usually stop there. My experience is that students continue to work on their own. Either they have spontaneously gone back to their families of origin and tried to reconnect with different members in different ways subsequently, or they have continued to think and remember incidents previously forgotten that demonstrate the existence of other parts of that family member that were previously denied. It starts a process of change to one's family of origin either in reality or fantasy. There is often follow-up in subsequent supervisory sessions, initiated by the student, which indicates the process of change has begun.

Students who have difficulty in thinking in circular terms regarding the etiology of family problems are often those in which there has been one idealized and one hated family member—one was all good and the other was all bad. Seeing their clients in three dimensions helps them begin to see these familial caricatures in three dimensions as well. When they do, it tends to unblock that learning difficulty, that of an inability to think in circular terms.

PSYCHIATRIC RESIDENT TRAINING

In the training of psychiatric residents the situation is somewhat different. There the students need to work together all week, there is a hierarchy from junior to senior to chief resident and they have not volunteered to learn family therapy but are obliged to have it as part

---

**It is most often the parents who are caricatured, though sometimes it is a sibling. For purposes of brevity I have called it—a parent.

of their training. Thus, building a trusting, cohesive group may be more of a problem. Self revelation may be much more threatening, and the teacher may be seen in a more judgmental frame because she is tied to an academic program which evaluates the student's capacity to become a psychiatrist. In the three year program the students already have a professional identity when they come.

Unless some of the students have had previous experience with the teacher and trust her, it will take much longer to arrive at the level of group cohesiveness necessary for family of origin work. If it works well, one group of residents will tell the next group and then the new group comes in asking for it. With psychiatric residents it is preferable to have the request for family of origin work come from them. That is an indication that they will be better prepared to benefit from it. The resident program is a didactic one, therefore my approach has been different in it. I usually ask the resident who has volunteered to present his family, to think about what is the problem he is having with his client families that he would like to focus on. He is asked to prepare the genogram at home so that he will have already started the process of self exploration. From there, the teaching is much the same as that described above except that it is more formal. He presents the genogram to the group, draws the lines and describes the relationships.

Members of the group are allowed to ask questions but there is a tacit understanding that it is the teacher who makes the links with the presenter, from his current problem as therapist to his family of origin. In this way, nobody plays psychiatrist and the presenter senses the respect with which his peers are treating the material. They remain in the student role. This has occurred spontaneously; they did not have to be told not to comment on colleagues' personal material during a family of origin session. I believe it is a result of waiting for a certain level of trust and respect to develop in the group before one starts work.

EXAMPLES

The following examples illustrate situations in which family of origin work was used. In the first, it was used as part of an ongoing supervision. In the second, it was used as part of a didactic teaching program. The goal is, of necessity, different in these two types of situations. When used as part of ongoing supervision the aim is to have a direct effect on the trainee's performance in a specific case which, hopefully, will spill over to other similar cases. When it is used as part of a didactic teaching program the purpose is more general. It is then used to increase the trainee's awareness that his relationship to members of his family of origin colours his perception of certain types of clients and limits his effectiveness as therapist with them. There is no follow-up as there is an ongoing supervision to help the trainee change his behaviour in relation to his patients. Caust et al.[5] have stated, "it is important that trainees be offered the opportunity to study their own families, both as a context for learning about family structure and function and as a vehicle for addressing the systemic countertransference issues that inevitably arise."

Example 1

Jacques was a 30 year old social worker who was having a great deal of difficulty in a client family in which the presenting problem was a 16 year old boy who was becoming increasingly involved in delinquent activities. The oldest of four, the boy had been a good student, easy to get along with at home and reasonably responsible. His behaviour had begun to change several years previously but the family did not come for help until he and a friend had been caught shoplifting and the police were involved. The father was a volatile man who worked long hours and was not very involved in the family's life. The mother was a warm, kind person who cried easily and was often bullied by her demanding, abrasive husband. The mother's health was poor, she tired easily, and the children often had to help when she became overwhelmed by her responsibilities. She claimed she could not turn to her husband at those times because he could not tolerate any demands on him and she was afraid of his temper. Jacques' perception of the father was that he was an infantile, deprived man in competition with his children, especially his oldest son, whom he saw as a rival for mother's affection. He thought father was subtly encouraging this boy to act out so that he should be punished and eventually sent away from home, thus eliminating him as a rival for mother. Despite Jacques' perception of father, he was able to empathize with his neediness. However, his sympathy for mother's plight, his great appreciation of her warmth and kindness made him unable to see the manipulative and aggressive way in which she kept her husband at a distance and kept the two men, her husband and son, vying for her attention. This was discussed in supervision and Jacques could not see it at all. He was also unable to see that any attempt on the son's part to become more autonomous resulted in a family crisis in which father threatened to become violent and son needed to stay home to "protect" mother. Jacques was not able to grasp that the son's increasingly delinquent behaviour might be very effective in forcing father to become involved in the family life in his role of parent, thus freeing son to continue the development appropriate to a 16 year old, and limiting mother's need to infantilize and "spousify" her oldest son.

After some time Jacques himself began to feel stuck with this case. It was not moving and he became increasingly frustrated and hopeless about his ability to be a family therapist. At this point I suggested some family of origin work. The supervisory group consisted of four people. This occurred in the second half of the year: the group had grown to like and trust each other enough that Jacques had no qualms agreeing to share his family of origin with the group. What emerged was that Jacques, though not the oldest, had been the son who had had the closest relationship with his mother. She had been a warm, nurturing woman with a heart condition. He had been very close to her and had tried to be helpful to her because he was afraid she might die. His father had been a quiet, rather depressed man who remained on the periphery of the family but one who worked hard to provide for them. Jacques' mother had died when he was a young adult and her loss had affected him deeply. In the discussion about his genogram he realized he had only dbegun to have a relationship with his father after his mother died. He had always thought his father had "mellowed" and become more approachable after his mother's death. It was only after this session that he began to have a notion that his mother had, in some way, kept his father apart from the children and that his father colluded with this because he cared about his wife and knew exclusive closencss with the children was important to her.

The session was a very moving one, Jacques cried and was able to admit that he wished he had had a well mother like other children had. It had been hard to live with the anxiety that if anything upset her, his mother might die; yet he could not be angry with her because she was so good and she certainly had not wanted to have a heart condition. The supervisor pointed out to Jacques that it was difficult for him to feel loving and angry with his mother at the same time. At this point the group was very helpful. They were supportive and accepting of the idea that one could have both positive and

negative feelings for the same person, indeed it was a natural phenomenon. The negative feelings did not have to be rational, they
were a consequence of a person's needs not having been met. This
non-blaming attitude on the part of the group was tantamount to
another "family" telling Jacques it was all right to have certain
unacceptable feelings.

This session seemed to unblock Jacques' difficulty not only in
dealing with his client's aggression, but also with his own. He was
gradually able to become much more appropriately confrontive in
his work. This session had not only helped him with this particular
family, but in his general therapeutic style.

Example 2

Jill was a 35 year old psychologist, in the third year of a three
year Family Therapy Training Program. She was known as a sensitive therapist who either did very well or very badly with her
cases. She lost a surprisingly large number of cases for her level of
skill. She volunteered to present her family of origin as part of the
didactic teaching out of intellectual curiosity. Jill did not present any
particular problem she had as a therapist but she had a vague feeling
of unease with certain kinds of men. She was not specific about what
kind of men she was referring to, nor what the feeling was. She was
currently treating a family where she had that feeling about the
father, with the result that she found herself avoiding him and dealing with the other family members.

Jill's genogram revealed two heavy lines from herself to her aunt
and to a sister. There was a wavy line between herself and her
mother, a disorganized, depressed woman who was unable to give
her children much mothering. However, the shock for Jill came
when she was totally unable to draw any kind of line between herself
and her father, yet she felt a strong connection with him. She could
not ignore it, insisting that there was a link between herself and him.
She wondered if it could be sexual but that did not feel correct to
her. She remained silent. The teacher then asked if she had any
memories involving her father which she would like to share with
the group. After a few minutes she described an incident where she
was walking home from school with a friend and saw her father, a
rag peddlar, being taunted by a group of children. Her first reaction
had been one of humiliation followed by a wish to comfort this
quiet, sad man who had never reached out to his children. However,

she was afraid that the taunting children would make fun of her too and that her school friend who belonged to a higher socioeconomic group, would want nothing to do with her when she realized who her father was. She ignored the scene and continued walking and chatting to her friend. She remembers feeling guilty about it when she got home, but neither she nor her father discussed it, even though she was quite sure he had seen her.

This memory was followed by silence. Jill slowly began to speak and said that she guessed she had a mixture of impatience and compassion for non-achieving men. It was hard for her to understand them. She also realized that she tended to see all passive men as having fewer resources than they had, even in situations where their success in their work or in the community belied their passivity and resourcelessness in the family. Jill was not in individual therapy: ideally, she should have gone into therapy because her conflictual feelings about her family were making it difficult for her to treat a wide spectrum of families. This session certainly helped her deal better with the father in the particular family she was treating. However, it was not therapeutic in that Jill's conflicts were too deep and needed to be dealt with in individual therapy. At this writing Jill has not gone into personal therapy but has changed her job so that she is doing more administration and less clinical work.

DISCUSSION

It is difficult to evaluate the effectiveness of family of origin work in training. Clearly that depends how, when and to what purpose it is used. My experience has been to use it as part of the supervision process as well as part of a didactic teaching program. My impression is that it is very helpful with some students, marginally helpful with others. I have not had an experience to date where it has been harmful. That is not to say that it has not sometimes been upsetting in the short run, but all countertransference awareness has that effect. It is important for the teacher to be free and available immediately after the session so that if there has been any feeling of distress in the group or in the presenter she is available to be supportive and caring. The availability of the teacher is very important in all training. Learning takes place in the context of a relationship between teacher and student. When that relationship is not nourishing and supportive it hinders the learning process. Whenever personal issues are touched upon, whether in individual or family therapy training, the student needs to feel the support and care of the teacher. This is especially true when these issues are discussed in a group and not in the privacy of a one to one supervisory relationship.

There are several recommendations that I would make so that family of origin work remains a training resource and does not become therapy.

1. The purpose should be clear and case related
2. There must be a high level of trust and respect in the group for each other and the teacher
3. Focus should be on the student's relationship to his family of origin and not his family of procreation
4. It should be time limited so that the focus can remain on training and not on therapy
5. Motivation is higher if the request for family of origin work comes from the students, rather than being imposed by the teacher
6. The teacher must have some time available after the session to deal with any unforeseen problem that might arise for the student presenter or the group.

This last point has been the reason many therapists do not think family of origin work should be included in a family therapy training program. They feel it belongs in therapy or as a growth experience for the therapist but that it is too risky to include in training. While this may be true, I believe that if the teacher is cautious and is available for a private follow-up if necessary, this is a resource that has a great deal to offer in the training of family therapists.

REFERENCES

1. Framo James L. A personal viewpoint on training in marital and family therapy. *Professional Psychology* 1979; 10, 868-75.
2. Napier Augustus, Whitaker Carl. Problems of the beginning family therapist. *Seminars in Psychiatry* 1973; 5:2.
3. Skynner Robin CA, Skynner Prudence. An open systems approach to teaching family therapy. *Journal of Marital and Family Therapy* 1979; 5 (4):5-16.
4. Ferber Andrew, Mendelssohn Marilyn. Training in family therapy. *Family Process* 1969; 8: 25-32.
5. Caust Barbara, Libow Judith, Raskin Pamela. Challenges and promises of training women as family systems therapists. *Family Process* 1981; 20 (4): 439-47.

The Supervision of Family of Origin Family Systems Treatment

Robert L. Beck

ABSTRACT. The primary emphasis in the Family of Origin Family Systems treatment literature is upon theory and treatment. A review of the existing literature reveals relatively little regarding the teaching or supervision of this model. The paper presents an integrative approach which includes theory, experiential learning and supervision. The author discusses candidacy criteria and preparation of the client for this treatment approach. Finally, case material is presented to describe the supervision and utilization of this model in practice.

The Family of Origin systems literature has described its application in numerous clinical, organizational and educational settings. Bowen meticulously details the theoretical underpinnings of the model (Bowen, 1978). Framo (1976), Williamson and Malone (1983), and The Georgetown Family Symposia collections (Lorio and McCullough, 1977; Sagar, 1978) describe Family of Origin systems approaches and their application to clinical practice. Two recently published articles address the issue of seeing the individual in family therapy (Kaplan, 1983; Petker, 1983). In one paper, Beck (in press) describes family interviews with clients and their parents in psychotherapy and in a second, presents a model for teaching family treatment through an integration of group process and systems' experiential work (Beck, 1982). McCullough's paper addresses the criteria for selecting individuals for Family of Origin family systems training (McCullough, 1978). Framo (1979) addresses the experiential component to his model of teaching family systems theory and stresses the importance of the trainees having

Robert L. Beck, M.A., C.S.W., is Chief Clinical Social Worker, Baylor Psychiatry Clinic, Assistant Professor, Department of Psychiatry, Baylor College of Medicine, Houston, Texas, and Adjunct Associate Professor, University of Houston, Graduate School of Social Work, Houston, Texas.

first hand knowledge and experiences of their family. In most of the Family of Origin literature, there resides an implication that it is sufficient to teach via the experience. While in all likelihood this is neither intended nor the reality, little exists in the literature to suggest otherwise.

This paper will address itself to teaching Family of Origin systems theory in social work education in an integrative way—utilizing didactic teaching and supervision. In the graduate education of clinical social workers, the instructor in the field or classroom faces a particular limitation which needs to be recognized and worked with from the outset. The social work student usually participates in the clinical practicum for no more than a nine month academic year. One of the two often unrelated field experiences, this clinical field placement comes in the second year of training and therefore does not afford the student or teacher opportunity to carry on the work for a second supervised year. The exposure to theory, experience and application must then be provided for a compacted nine month period. While the work will hopefully go on, it is incumbent upon the instructor to approach the teaching with some precision and focus, and to offer a relatively brief but intense experience for the student.

The emphasis here will be upon the integration of theory, personal experience and practice that must take place while addressing the supervision of the students' work with his clients who will venture into their own families of origin. Given a nine month limitation of time, the model to be described provides a two-step process, that of learning the treatment material, followed by the experiential phase, with an overlaying of the clinically supervised application to work with clients during the second phase as described in an earlier paper (Beck, 1983).

A TRAINING MODEL

This approach to supervision presupposes that the student is concurrently participating in, or had previously participated in, a supervised individual or group family of origin experience. As illustrated in an earlier paper, an integrated group and family systems approach can be utilized to provide experiential learning which can serve as the foundation upon which the student can build the clinical work with his or her own clients (Beck, 1982). The author has found this experiential approach to be most effective and meaningful in teaching these concepts, and to ensure a solid integration of the theory. The model provides a time-limited group experience in which theory is presented in the first quarter of the experience. The group then addresses itself to the members' family of origin through a meticulous study of the individual's role in his or her family. Based upon previously established goals, the group member sets about the task of determining the focus of his re-entry into the family system. For Bowen's family systems theory and approach, the student works toward developing one-to-one connections or relationships with significant family members, and in maintaining differentiation within his or her family of origin.

This re-entry into the family is achieved through written contact, phone contact, and periodic home visits in which the student member "experiments" in maintaining the differentiated position within the family. The instructor/consultant, not true to a classical Bowen approach, addresses the group as a whole, regarding its group anxiety, dependency, and rage (Beck, 1982).

As is evident here, the student is therefore given opportunities to understand himself within the family, and to do so in the context of a growing understanding of the family of origin concepts. The instructor serves both as a consultant to the individual student, to the group, and to the group process that can both support and potentially inhibit the individual student's ability to continue to address the task. The student ultimately begins to engage his or her individual patients or clients and family of origin work concurrent with continuing experiential work with fellow students. The bulk of this paper will address itself to supervision of graduate students of social work in family of origin clinical practice.

APPLICATION TO PRACTICE

Given the students' didactic and experiential exposure to family of origin family systems theory as described above, they begin to develop an understanding of the potential for application of these concepts in their clinical work. Family of origin work with clients is most effectively introduced after the students' presentation of their own family to the seminar group, and have begun to identify their role in their family system, their level of differentiation with particular family members, and set goals for their relationship. With the assistance of the supervisor, the students begin to identify the way in which the current family issues play a continuing role in the client's maintenance of the symptomatic behavior. At the outset of the students' work with individual clients or couples, the student is encouraged to develop a genogram with the assistance of the patient regardless of the orientation of the treatment. The student has therefore entered the treatment process with the client within the context of some understanding of the nature of the family and has set the stage for possible continued exploration within the family system.

IDENTIFICATION OF THE FAMILY OF ORIGIN CANDIDATE

Criteria for Appropriateness

The following six criteria are considered by this author to be essential for initially engaging the patient in family of origin family systems approach within the context of dynamically oriented psychotherapy: 1) The client must be in pain—that is, the patient must be experiencing personal conflicts or concerns, and express motivation to change. 2) The client has successfully identified issues with the therapist that suggest fusion or enmeshment in the family, and presents difficulties in assuming a differentiated position with particular family members. 3) The existence of a therapeutic alliance. The demands of this approach involve considerable trust that the consultant or therapist will remain available and provide assistance through the client's often frightening re-entry into the family. 4) The existence of a non-chaotic life style—simply, the client must not exhibit self destructive behavior and must be able to maintain some task orientation. 5) A demonstrated ability to cognitively connect the past to the present—here the client must demonstrate some capacity to see the connectedness between past and current family interactions to the present expressed concerns. 6) Finally, willingness to work within this framework. The client must express a willingness to re-enter his family in a new way with the assistance of the therapist.

Items 2, 4, and 6 are particularly important to the application of family of origin family systems work and are not necessarily requirements in most other psychotherapies. Our students, early in their skill development, cannot carry the day by charisma alone, and need as much supportive underpinnings for the initial therapeutic work as are necessary. The author therefore suggests that these six criteria are essential for the initial development of the therapeutic alliance and treatment and particularly where this approach is integrated into a psychodynamic framework.

Preparing the Client for Family of Origin Work

Once appropriateness for family of origin work is determined, the student is asked to teach the basic components of the family of origin family systems model to the client. Three concepts in particular are discussed and are related to the client's own family system. The first of these concepts is that of triangles, the second, multi-generational transmission process, and the third, family projection process. The client is encouraged to describe existing triangles and patterns of triangling in his or her family system after the therapist has illustrated the process using examples related to friendship patterns and dyadic relationships. The therapist describes the triangling process as basic to what goes awry in family systems and indicates that shared but non-verbalized discomfort in dyadic relationships, is often diffused by focusing on a third party or issue, i.e. a child, and this is illustrated by a triangle in the client's own family system. The fluidity of triangles is described to the client in order to relate non-ending work required in maintaining a differential position. Finally, the multi-generational transmission process is described in order to brief the client on the possibility that what he or she is experiencing in the family is a function of a long history of unresolved family tensions, and underscores the importance of both returning home and gathering history, or in order to work toward resolution of the perceived discomfort regarding the family. Finally, the therapist talks with the client about the nature of one-to-one relationships, and the difficulty in sustaining a one-to-one connection with family members or in one's own family system.

The second stage of client preparation involves the development of the genogram or family tree. The development of the genogram is an important tool in defining the family issues and understanding the client's role in the family system. Obvious omissions, spottiness of information, or lack of data regarding a family member who is still living and presumably accessible to the patient, are all explored. The client's own anxieties about connecting with these particular family members or prohibitions in the family regarding the same are also identified.

The student is forewarned that as the client begins to re-enter the family, he will come back frustrated, empty, disappointed or angry that so little material has been offered. The student therapist is instructed to provide a supportive, understanding milieu in which information, or lack thereof, is seen as important data in helping the two understand the nature of the family system. The development of the genogram as well as the delineation of the triangles and differentiation issues, all serve as a backdrop for the setting of specific behavioral changes which the client and therapist will define.

Once there has been mutual exploration of the client's own perceptions of his or her role in the structure of the family system, the student therapist is instructed to begin to help the client define specific changes or expectations regarding the family system. In tune with the earlier discussions of the nature of triangling or differentiation of self issues within the family, the client is assisted in defining his or her role in the maintenance of particular triangling patterns within the family system. The family of origin family systems work is geared heavily toward the client thinking, rather than feeling, his or her way through change. The client must be assisted in maintaining a participant/observer status within the family, while at the same time maintaining some degree of anxiety in order to stimulate motivation for change.

The shift from learning the theory and examining the nature of the family to moving within the family in a new way is often fraught with great resistance and anxiety. Moving the therapeutic work out of the relatively safe therapist/client alliance is a major step for the client and must be supported by the belief that the therapist will be there as the family system is re-entered.

Case One

> Joyce, a second year graduate student in Social Work, had previously discussed the possibility of engaging her client, Susan, in Family of Origin Work. Susan, a 29-year old divorced woman, had presented to the clinic with depressive symptoms, difficulties in maintaining a desired weight without the assistance of diet pills, and a chronic pattern of difficulties in maintaining appropriate relationships with available, unmarried men. The supervisor and Joyce had tentatively discussed a plan which would include the development of a genogram, examination of the existing triangles within Susan's family of origin and finally, conceptualization of Susan's difficulties in family system's terms. The latter would hopefully serve as a link to

understanding Susan's difficulties within the context of continuing family of origin interventions and set the stage for future intervention.

In a subsequent session, Susan informed Joyce that her mother was coming for a visit and Joyce immediately suggested to an ambivalent Susan that she bring her mother in for an interview. Joyce's enthusiasm was in part a function of her relative inexperience and magical wish that a therapeutic reunion would solve all. She had not laid the ground work with her client, leaving Susan unprepared, but passively agreeable to the proposed interview. Susan's need to please, in collusion with Joyce's need to succeed, led the two into a rather unproductive, tense and loosely focused interview. While the interview was instructive, it was minimally productive.

This case describes the rather abrupt entry of the patient and student social worker into the world of the family with minimal preparatory work. While the outcome of such interventions can be instructive and helpful diagnostically, they potentially threaten the client-therapist alliance and can ultimately serve as a definitive influence on future well-timed entries into the family. Joyce's response to the client underscores the importance of the supervisory monitoring of the family of origin work.

Case Two

John, a second year graduate student in social work, began to present his work with Beverly, a 27-year old gay woman with whom he had been working individually. Beverly's parents, both dead, were survived by a maternal grandmother, a matriarch who had maintained a strong influence on Beverly's rearing and was currently a powerful influence on her. Dynamically, the grandmother had been serving as a representation of Beverly's parental dyad as was evidenced by her continuing ambivalent feelings about her influence in her life. Beverly was unable to attach comfortably or detach in an unambivalent manner. Her waxing and waning about her grandmother was reflected by her equally ambivalent relationship with her lover, a young woman whose own personal struggle was symbolized by her bisexuality.

John approached the family of origin work with Beverly in a

meticulous, directive manner, developed a broadened geno-gram, examined Beverly's current triangled relationships with the patient, and developed a mutually acceptable conceptual-ization of her ambivalence. The link to grandmother was ex-plored and Beverly ultimately decided to alter the way she related to her grandmother. A plan of intervention was deter-mined which included some initial explorative journeys into the relationship by letter and the process was begun with a shared sense of commitment and direction.

It is obvious that John stood a better chance of engaging Beverly in this family systems work, considering the well thought through and carefully monitored approach which was utilized.

The First Entry into the Family

Following the development of the genogram, and the determina-tion of the goals for family intervention, the student therapist begins to define the interventive framework with the client. Interventions are geared to the client's level of anxiety about entering into the family system, the degree of emotional cut-off from the family member in question, the level of trust in the therapist and the pro-cess, the nature and structure of the family and, of course, to the desired changes on the part of the patient. The supervisor's theoret-ical understanding and creativity will come heavily into play at this stage. Given the numerous factors impinging upon the therapeutic process, it is not possible to offer a hard and fast strategy for all family interventions.

The client who presents the family system with a great degree of vagueness, and whose own historical understanding is vague would be urged to initially go about gathering significant data in order to flesh out the skeletal presentation. The following case description will illustrate the supervisory relationship and its effect on the pro-gression from educating the patient to data gathering to more specif-ic interventions aimed at altering the structure of the child-parent dyad.

Case Three

Frank, in his live supervised work with a couple in marital treatment, began to help them move beyond the projections and blaming of one another to a point where each was beginning to identify personal conflicts as they affected the marriage. Supervision was live, utilizing a oneway mirror. The supervisor and student had established a good working alliance as had the student with the couple. The thrust of treatment had been problem solving and dynamically based until it became evident that re-entry into the emotional sphere of the families-of-origin would be helpful.

The couple had married at a time when each felt intense desires to extricate themselves from their families. In retrospect, both looked back upon their childhood and adolescence as filled with disappointment, anger at their parents, and a sense that the only way out was through a new attachment. She had become pregnant, they married, and neither considered other alternatives.

The husband's primary complaints centered around his wife's demands for communication and closeness, her anger, and withholding sex. Her complaints centered around his withholding nature, unwillingness to communicate with her, and demands for sex. He saw her as demanding, volatile and emotionally needy—all attributes of his mother. She saw him as aloof, withholding, unavailable—all attributes of her father.

Neither had successfully exited their families of origin; they entered the marriage to avoid confronting their disappointment with their respective parents. Once a commitment to the marriage was established, and the nature of the projections understood, each was encouraged to consider the impact of their emotional cut-off on the marital conflict. The student was encouraged to assist the individual spouses in establishing a more productive link to the appropriate parents. As the student has limited exposure to this family systems model, and the focus of treatment had initially been problem solving, the supervisor thought it best to take a more active role by entering the therapy room as a consultant.

Each spouse defined specific goals regarding shifts in their relationship with the parent with whom they felt the most significant cut-off. The wife chose her father, whom she saw as inaccessible. His inaccessibility was, in her view, a result of his need to distance and her mother's role as gatekeeper to the relationship. This served to protect father as well as guarantee mother's role as mother to her children. The wife initially approached the father by letter in which she reviewed the nature of their relationship and indicated a wish for increased communication. The supervisor suggested that the expressed wish not indicate closeness as the goal; as the threat to the marital system was deemed too great. The wife wrote, heard nothing for two weeks and was then, at the supervisor's suggestion, encouraged to call her father. The call was interrupted by her mother who admonished her daughter for "upsetting" her father. The mother also indicated that at that moment her father was resting (he had a heart condition) and was best not disturbed.

It was predictable that the mother would impede her daughter's access to the father and the therapist was prepared to suggest that the daughter begin to manage her relating to her mother somewhat differently. The supervisory process addressed the student's uncertainty about the process and the supervisor continued to advise, illustrate and encourage the student's creative use of himself as the drama unfolded. As the process moved beyond data gathering and the patient was needing more direction, the student was encouraged to examine the nature of the triangles with the client and to help the patient define her desired position in her family. She was asked to both increase her phone contact with her mother as she stepped up her correspondence with her father in an effort to not solely threaten her uneasy alliance with her mother as she reached out to her father. As her mother's anxiety about being displaced could easily upset the daughter's attempts to dialogue with her father, it was suggested that she maintain a continuous one-to-one pattern of relating to her mother focused on their relationship. Once the process had begun, the student had become more active in the sessions, indicating his increasing confidence and clarity of purpose, the supervisor returned to behind the one-way screen.

In this instance, the supervisor assumed a consultative role to both the student and the couple and in so doing, served as a model for future intervention. As this particular couple had been treated initially via a communication and psycho-dynamically oriented approach, the transition to a more directive approach required the supervisor to enter the treatment experience more directly and model in process. The interventions were not processed postmortem and then reinstituted; rather, the supervisor nudged the patient-student system through direct teaching and then exited once the process had begun.

SUMMARY

The author has described a supervisory/consultative process in the teaching of family of origin family systems theory and practice which incorporates didactically delivered material, an experiential family of origin group and supervised clinical practice. As described, the supervisory relationship is a difficult one to negotiate and maintain as the supervisor's role involves classical teaching, experiential small group leadership and case supervision. It has been suggested that the supervisor ultimately serves as the integrative link for the student between the theory, increased self awareness and clinical application.

The model establishes the supervisor as a consultant, teacher and classical supervisor as the treatment unfolds. As indicated earlier, the supervisor's task includes the introduction of a form of intervention which can be integrated into a dynamically oriented therapy but initially requires a more directive approach on the part of the student. Therefore, the supervisor will be required to assume a less reflective stance in order to instruct and model so as to encourage this increased activity level on the part of the student.

As four relationship systems are involved in this teaching approach—the student/client relationship, the client/family relationship, the student and his own family relationship and the supervisory relationship, a primary task for the supervisor is the appropriate maintenance of these systems. Fortunately, he has the assistance of the student's hopefully intense desire to learn and be therapeutically effective, as well as the client or family's interest in change. With so many working so diligently, the task will in all likelihood be realized.

REFERENCES

Beck, R.L. Beyond the Transference: Adults and their Parents in Psychotherapy, *Clinical Social Work Journal*, in press.

Beck, R.L. Process and Content in the Family of Origin Group, in *International Journal of Group Psychotherapy*, 1982, *32*(2), 233-244.

Beck, R.L. Teaching Family Systems Theory: A Group Experience in the Field. Paper presented at the Fifth Annual Symposium of the Committee for the Advancement of Social Work with Groups, Detroit, 1983.

Bowen, M. *Family Therapy in Clinical Practice.* New York: Aronson, 1978.

Framo, J.L. A Personal Viewpoint on Training in Marital and Family Therapy. *Professional Psychology*, 1979, *10*, 868-875.

Framo, J.L. Family of Origin as a Therapeutic Resource for Marital and Family Therapy: You Can and Should Go Home Again. *Family Process*, 1976, *15*, 193-210.

Kaplan, B.E. The Individual and the Extended Family in Family Therapy. *The Family,* 1983, 10(2), 94-99.

Lorio, J.P. & McClenathan, L. (Ed.) *Georgetown Family Symposia,* (Vol. II). Washington, D.C.: Georgetown University, 1977.

McCullough, P.G. Assessing Motivation to Work on Extended Family. R.R. Sagar (Ed.), *Georgetown Family Symposia,* (Vol. III). Washington, D.C.: Georgetown University, 1978.

Petker, S. Seeing the Individual with Family Members. *The Family,* 1983, *10,* (2), 115-121.

Sagar, R.R. (Ed.) *Georgetown Family Symposia,* A Collection of Selected Papers (Vol. III). Washington D.C.: Georgetown University, 1978.

Williamson, D.S., and Malone, P.E. Systems-Oriented, Small Group, Family of Origin Family Therapy: A Comparison with Traditional Group Psychotherapy. *Journal of Group Psychotherapy, Psychodrama and Sociometry,* Winter, 1983, 165-177.

Uses and Abuses
of Family of Origin Material
in Family Therapy Supervision

Carlton E. Munson

ABSTRACT. There has been a parallel increase in family therapy practice and emphasis on family of origin material among social work students and practitioners. There has been no concomitant assessment of the use of family of origin material as a tool used in supervision. This article traces the evolution of family of origin material and how it must be applied differentially to promote learning about family practice.

INTRODUCTION

There is no doubt that clinical social work practice is widespread and extensive in the delivery of psychotherapeutically-oriented services in the United States. Social workers are the largest single group delivering psychotherapy services in the United States (Sobel, 1980:3). Social workers are the largest professional group that make up the staff of mental health centers in this country. There is at the same time much interest in family therapy on the part of these practitioners as well as among clinical social work students that are the overwhelming majority in graduate schools of social work. In spite of this increased clinical practice activity, there have been few articles that have evaluated techniques used in clinical practice or supervision. There is no widespread effort to evaluate clinical social work practice. By and large the social work profession only pays lip service to research in practice.

In the practice of psychotherapy today the range of interventions available are diverse indeed. Clients can expect anything from masturbation, to sexual intercourse, to a therapist who will barely speak to them (Langs, 1982:7). Therapists in supervision are slightly bet-

---

Carlton E. Munson, D.S.W., is Associate Professor, Graduate School of Social Work, University of Houston, Houston, Texas 77004.

ter off than their clients. Just as there are no real standards for what constitutes good practice, there are no guidelines for good supervision. In a field that has over 300 competing theories, little scientific foundation, and vague qualifications for practice, there is little wonder that what one experiences in supervision in analogous to a termite in a yo-yo. In a field that has been described as in "chaos" (Langs, 1982:9), supervisees are by and large at the mercy of their supervisors when it comes to enhancing their practice skills. There is a growing concern about how supervisees can be victimized by their supervisors unwittingly (Langs, 1982).

This problematic supervisory situation is especially apparent in family therapy supervision, and it is this area that will be the focus of this paper. This author began to question the use of family of origin material when problems with it emerged in the comments made by MSW students who were participating in a research project that involved in-depth content analysis of the supervision the students were undergoing. As a result of the students' comments in this study, it was decided to explore the issue of family of origin material in supervision.

Langs has identified what he calls the "therapeutic conspiracy" in which both the therapist and the patient use strategies to avoid promoting therapeutic change. Supervisors and supervisees concomitantly engage in what can be referred to as the "educational conspiracy" to avoid supervisory interaction that will promote exploration of effective intervention strategies. Family of origin groups that focus on exploration of therapist family dynamics is one form of educational conspiracy. Groups with such focus allow the supervisor and supervisee to deal with material that has little real relationship to the clinical cases the supervisee is faced with in practice. Family of origin groups can be helpful as a learning tool, but when the educational objective is diminished and replaced with a therapeutic focus, problems can emerge. This paper deals with identifying and preventing lapsing into the educational conspiracy.

FAMILY THERAPY SUPERVISION
AND FAMILY OF ORIGIN MATERIAL

The literature on family therapy is confusing for the beginning therapist and can leave them with the impression that "everything seems to work" (Kramer, 1980:281). This holds true in training to be a family therapist. Younger therapists are likely to have been exposed to family therapy theory and concepts as part of their professional training, but such exposure is often less than adequate and entered upon before the practitioner is skilled at performing individual or group therapy (Kramer, 1980:275-276).

There seems to be general agreement that personal therapy associated with exploration of the therapist's own family dynamics leads to one being a better family therapist. Therapists are encouraged to enter therapy to enhance their professional performance, and family therapy supervisors are encouraged to "openly discuss with students their experiences in current relationships with their own families" as a model for their supervisees' own practice (Goldenberg and Goldenberg, 1980:234-235). Kramer has argued that " . . . the family therapist who has not worked on his own family relationships" is "handicapped" (Kramer, 1980:298).

Given these theoretical views about the importance of personal life experience to learning to do family therapy, the confusion about what constitutes good treatment, and the lack of adequate practice experience in doing family therapy on the part of beginning practitioners, most inexperienced practitioners naturally have a tendency to commit to any strategy or technique that will aid them in coping with demanding and complex practice material.

The use of family of origin material represents one of these learning strategies that holds up exploration of personal experience as a means to learn about practice. This expectation is developed early in a therapist's career during the training stage. One report in the literature of the use of family of origin material in a social work classroom setting illustrates this (Magee, 1982:14-19). The report reflects a trend to personalize for the student various forms of course content. This is done based on the notion that having the student draw on personal experience to understand conceptual material fosters integration of content, development of self-awareness, and promotes learning. While this makes for elegant prose about educational methodology, there is no empirical evidence to support the view that this is the most effective and efficient way to promote learning. There has not been any consideration that the use of such techniques may impede learning and violate students' right to privacy.

In the project cited above, the teacher attempted to integrate research content and human behavior and social environment content (HBSE), two non-practice oriented areas, through *requiring* the students to do research on their own families and do written reports as well as class presentations of their "findings." The instructor in this social work class considered such topics as religion, sex, work, health, assertiveness and money potentially "toxic." The teacher/ author goes on to discuss examples of "toxic" issues that equal any content explored during intensive family therapy. Even though this exercise used in an HBSE course is described as a "substantive research project," there is no mention of evaluation of the exercise and student feedback about being compelled to reflect upon and reveal to others such sensitive, personal experiences. Such exploration of students' personal lives to promote learning under any circumstances is, in my opinion, unjustified. Haley has succinctly stated my point of view on such practices by observing that supervisees' lives are too important to be tampered with by supervisors (Haley, 1976:187).

The only report of use of FOO groups in the field component in social work education was reported by Thistle (1981). She holds that students believe that " . . . unashamed inquiry in these [family] relationships is not only helpful but essential to the development of the family therapist." The author goes on to make the bold assertion, "The modification of the trainee's role in his or her own family is one of the most dramatic and effective ways of teaching family therapy" (Thistle, 1981:248). Given these two statements, a basic contradiction emerges from the article that is not addressed by the author. This contradiction is that the patients of the agency, where the family of origin group was used, are severely mentally ill people who need inpatient psychiatric treatment, and their backgrounds are substantially different from the backgrounds of the therapist trainees. In spite of these major differences, the trainees purported to learn about their clients through presenting "family albums and records and genograms" that make " . . . the families come alive for group members" (Thistle, 1981:249). This type exploration is justified on the grounds that "The individual attracted to the helping professions is often more comfortable looking at someone else's problems than his or her own" (Thistle, 1981:249). This view becomes the basis for the assertion that the main "task" of the group is for the trainee " . . . to develop skills as researchers in their own families" (Thistle, 1981:249). We are never told how this relates to or what it has to do with what the trainee does with his or her own patients.

This issue is not only whether students should be compelled to reveal personal information in training programs, but also whether they should even be allowed to do it voluntarily. People talking about their personal problems generally has nothing to do with their own learning about doing good treatment.

HISTORY OF FAMILY OF ORIGIN IN SUPERVISION

Unlike many therapy techniques, the history of the use of family of origin material can be traced. It originated with Murray Bowen. The evolution of Bowen's ideas in this area are explained in his book, *Family Therapy in Clinical Practice* (1978). There is a rather elaborate interweaving of points in the last fifty pages of the book that describe this evolution. Bowen reports he first learned to apply therapeutic dynamics to his family from a sickness perspective during his early psychoanalytic training. Later he began using his own theoretical formulations to study his own family. He worked through this by writing lengthy letters to his parents and siblings and calculated mailing them to coincide with trips to visit his family. This caused members of his family much anguish, and he reports one brother was so angered he threatened a libel suit (Bowen, 1978:513). While these letters and visits eventually resulted in Bowen achieving much contentment, his family remained in conflict and confused by his actions.

In 1967 Bowen began using his own family of origin experiences to teach psychiatric residents about treatment. These residents began using these examples with their own families, and Bowen observes that these residents appeared to be "doing better clinical work as family therapists than any previous residents" (Bowen, 1978:531). Bowen began treating residents using this approach. He reports there was one "control" group in which he focused on extended family material, but admits the results were disappointing. Bowen has continued to use these techniques with residents and their wives as part of the training program at Georgetown. Hundreds of therapists have gone to Georgetown and participated in these training seminars. Many psychotherapists from various disciplines now use family of origin groups to train other therapists. They use the same techniques with their own supervisees that Bowen demonstrated and used with them, including exploration of family of origin material and letter writing exercises.

There have been no empirical tests of what Bowen has produced as a participant observer in his own training seminars (Gurman, 1981:355). No specific guidelines for the use of FOO material with therapists in training have been developed. There are no reports in the literature of positive or negative outcomes or misapplications of this approach. While reports occur in the literature identifying problems, there has been a tendency to overlook them and emphasize the positive assumptions of the approach (see Gurman, 1981:352-364).

The author attended one training session conducted by two therapists/supervisors trained by Bowen where they provided an elaborate explanation of Bowen's theory based on general systems theory. Bowen has publically stated that his formulations are not based on general systems theory (Bowen, 1978:398). This is a rather innocuous but basic error that causes one to ask if more harmful errors are being made as sensitive family material is explored with unwitting, and sometimes unwilling, supervisees. Such misrepresentations can be attributed to a general lack of understanding of theory that supervisors and supervisees are attempting to use in relation to clinical learning. In such situations it appears the focus of supervision is allowed to stray and be directed at therapist dynamics rather than patient functioning.

In some of the case examples that follow, it would appear that some questionable applications of this material is taking place.

CASE EXAMPLES

One case example that illustrates the lack of differential applications of FOO material is illustrated by a student therapist I will call Mary. Mary was a second-year graduate student in an outpatient mental health clinic where her supervisor was a strong advocate of FOO groups for practitioners, and the supervisor had participated in several institutes at Georgetown University conducted by Murray Bowen. The supervisor urged her supervisees to participate in a FOO group she conducted. Mary moved into one of these groups, and after several sessions was encouraged to present her family. Mary presented her father as an aloof, stern businessman who did not communicate much. When her father tried to talk with her, Mary's mother would always interfere and accuse them of "plotting against her." Mary's mother had a life-long history of mental illness and had a series of hospitalizations. In order to avoid his wife's wrath, Mary's father was portrayed as giving up on trying to communicate with Mary, which Mary found depressing, but at the same time felt anger at her father for not confronting his wife with her "unfounded" accusations. Mary left home over ten years ago and had visited her parents infrequently since leaving home. Mary had one younger sister who had not attended college and "has never found her place in life." In recent years her parents, who live over 1,500 miles away, were described as having settled into complacency about their life situation and acceptance of their daughter's loss of contact with them. Her parents remained reservedly proud of Mary's accomplishments. Mary desired to relate to her parents in a different way but did not know how to achieve this.

The FOO group convinced Mary she was engaged in a classic triangle with her parents and encouraged her to write a letter to her parents explaining this triangle and indicate she wanted to break up this pattern of relating. After a holiday visit home, Mary, with much ambivalence, prepared a letter she read to the group and subsequently mailed to her parents. The parents wrote back indicating they did not understand Mary's comments, but they still loved her and would like to fly in for her graduation because they were proud of her accomplishments. Mary took her parents' letter back to the FOO group and was advised by the group to write her parents indicating she would refuse to see them if they came for her graduation, and that her achieving a graduate degree had been accomplished alone without help from them. It was the group's view that this would be a good way to break up the old pattern of "triangling." Mary followed through on this with another letter. The parents responded again with a long letter professing their love for her, their lack of understanding about her position, but that they would honor her feelings and not attend the graduation.

The question remains whether this was the best and appropriate way to deal with Mary's situation, but the more important question is what this had to do with Mary's own development as a family therapist, and none of it was ever related by the group to her own family practice. It is my view that this was an unwarranted and unjustified intrusion into Mary's personal life.

In groups where family of origin material is explored extensively, it can become intertwined with group process and group dynamics which can give rise to therapeutic difficulties. Beck (1982a) has reported an example of this where a group member became reluctant to explore family of origin material, and this in turn gave rise to "considerable resentment on the part of other group members."

This reaction of the group lead the patient (we are not told if these patients were therapists themselves in a supervision group) to withdraw from the group. The question that emerges from this case example is: What is to become of such participants who exercise their right of self-determination and do not agree to such a course of treatment or supervision? For supervisors who use family of origin material in learning situations, the rules or conditions for trainee withdrawal from exposure of personal content should be made clear when the supervision process is initiated.

The following case example illustrates how resistance can be problematic for the therapist in supervision:

> I was only married six months when my supervisor required me to participate in a family of origin group she was conducting. I didn't know much about it, but I thought I would give it a try. My husband is very involved with his family. This didn't particularly bother me, but the group pressed me about it. I've talked to my husband about it, but without much enthusiasm. He isn't into psychology, and he discounts this stuff. I did it because the group pushed me about it. I regret having done it. I want this marriage to work. It's the second marriage for both of us. My husband doesn't understand what I'm going through. I wish I would never have brought it up. I don't think it's that important. I don't see what it has to do with learning to do good therapy. I feel comfortable with our relationship as it is. I'm being more cautious about what I reveal in the group, but I can sense some of the other members don't like the way I'm reacting.

Supervisees become frustrated and disoriented when they fail to see the connection between actions of the family of origin group and their own families. Such experiences cause the therapist in training to become resentful and to view such efforts as being involuntarily forced into personal therapy. Without adequate safeguards, personalizing family of origin material for the supervisee is a return to the former problematic practice of "psychologizing" the worker. Also, in situations like this, the therapist's learning is blocked because so much energy goes into resisting the group. When this occurs, the main objective of family of origin groups is thwarted—the supervisee ceases to learn about family therapy and how to become more skilled at doing it.

There is inconsistency in the logic in use by some who advocate family of origin work for therapy trainees. For example, Braverman (1982) advocates the use of this method based on a statement of James Framo that "when we train students formally we continue the training they got from their parents, brothers, sisters, grandparents, aunts and uncles." Several paragraphs later she states that in her own supervision using family of origin groups the student " . . . is not asked about . . . his family of procreation because this is not the cause of his difficulty with his clients and also because that would be unnecessarily intrusive" (Braverman, 1982:630). This observation is confusing on three counts. First, if Framo's logic of continuity is valid, why is the family of procreation considered null and void? Is it not a part of the person's continuity of life development? Second, if the family of procreation is sacrosanct, why is the family of origin not also inviolate? The logic of right to freedom of intrusion does not have a rational basis in one instance and not the other. Third, it is not clear how the supervisor can be so certain the supervisee's "difficulty with clients" is lodged in the family of origin and not the family of procreation. In fact, if Framo's notion holds, the difficulty would be *more likely,* rather than less likely, to appear in this area.

Framo's view aside, there is no scientific basis for the assumption that problems of the student therapist can only arise from the family of origin. Are we to believe that a practitioner whose wife was killed in an auto accident involving a drunk driver will find solace for his grief in his family of origin where he experienced an alcoholic father? The issues are often more complex than the "family of originists" would have us believe. Until these gaps in logic and complex issues are resolved, we must proceed with caution regarding the use of this method as a training tool.

Difficulty can occur when practitioners are participants in family of origin supervisory groups and simultaneously undergoing serious personal problems. Supervisees in this situation have a tendency to engage in half-veiled efforts to get help from the supervisory group and delay getting genuine therapy for themselves. Such delays can exacerbate emotional problems, affect the potential for positive outcome of treatment, and can result in increased problems for supervisees and their own family members. When a therapist is in crisis is not the time to explore his or her family background (Carter and McGoldrick, 1980:340). The supervisor must be vigilant about early signs of personal stress in supervisees and direct about supervisees' need for treatment. There is research evidence that professionals are extremely reluctant to confront even serious, prolonged dysfunctional behavior in colleagues and supervisees (Bissell et al., 1980).

As people age reminiscence in service of the ego increases in importance. When older therapists in training are involuntarily compelled to use family of origin material as a negative experience to learn, it can be detrimental to the trainee. The literature on use of family of origin material in supervision implies that the focus is on the defective aspects of past family experiences. More emphasis needs to be placed on the positive elements of family of origin material and how this can be used to enhance learning for practice.

FAMILY OF ORIGIN MATERIAL AND PRACTICE

The effect of family of origin emphasis in supervision has not been assessed from the perspective of its influence on practice activity. It has been shown that rarely is family of origin material applied in the supervision of the practitioner as it relates to the practitioner's clinical activity. Where this gap exists the potential is created for the practitioner to misapply this material with their cases. There must be follow up of such learning and its application as well as clinical demonstration of its relevance to clinical situations.

If countertransference is a valid psychodynamically oriented psychotherapy phenomenon, it must be kept in mind by the supervisor that it occurs only in the context of patient dynamics. If this basic premise is accepted, and it is not apparent how it could not be, then use of family of origin material must be explored in relation to the patient dynamics that gave rise to the countertransference in conjunction with the therapist in supervision. Because of this inherent connection between patient and therapist dynamics, family of origin material must always be case related.

Also, overemphasis on family of origin material in supervision can lead the practitioner to a disproportionate focus on such material in cases. Dwelling on such material can fascinate, but can lead to a narrow focus that detracts from a problem focus in the treatment. It can result in focusing on historical and inactive relationships at the expense of current relationship issues. Tangible concrete problems and dysfunctional interactional and communication patterns in the family can be overlooked and avoided. This is especially the case in the diagnostic phase of intervention. This is illustrated by a student trainee in family of origin oriented supervision who presented a case she was treating through elaborate genograms tracing the family history of alcoholism back to the post Civil War era. After a half hour presentation, the supervisor asked the trainee what she was going to do to help the family, and the trainee responded, "I am not sure." If assessment of the family functioning is inadequate, limited, and not treatment focused, then the treatment will necessarily be distorted and misguided.

At the same time, old, dormant, inactive triangles in the therapist's personal life should not be reestablished as part of the supervision. Such actions should remain in the realm of therapy. The triangles in the family being treated by the practitioner should be the focus in the supervision. It has been pointed out that the essence of family therapy is focus "on actual behavior, what is observably going on in the present, rather than on the past, the internal and the inferential" (Fisch et al., 1982:8-9). This should be the focus of supervision to integrate diagnosis and treatment activities of the therapist.

Supervision should focus on the interventions to be made by the therapist. To focus in supervision on the supervisee and his or her own life experience is to engage in what was referred to earlier as Langs' (1982) characterization of "The Psychotherapeutic Conspiracy." Langs has appropriately pointed out that the therapist's personal experiences elicited by the supervisor has more to do with the supervisee's reaction to the supervisor than to anything that exists in clients the supervisee treats, and supervisees in such a supervisory situation are at the mercy of an often unsympathetic supervisor (Langs, 1982:18-19).

These issues remain unexplored in the use of family of origin material. Supervisors who insist upon its use must be aware of these problems and develop strategies to combat such problems. Beck (1982b), in the only specific analysis of the use of family of origin groups in supervision, has articulated methods to prevent some of the abuses that have been identified here. Supervisors need to explore alternate means of promoting effective family treatment. For example, are there alternate methods of exploring family of origin material that put practitioners at less risk personally and are at the same time more practice relevant? Also, supervisors need to ask whether other practice methods are as effective, or more effective, in encouraging quality practice. For example, can the same ends be achieved through the use of cotherapists in family treatment? More attention needs to be given to appropriate differential application of family of origin material to practice situations. Beck (1982a) has alluded to the shortcoming of family of origin material in some situations.

In analyzing therapy practice three points of view are important: (1) the therapeutic person, (2) the therapeutic modality, and (3) the therapeutic context (Wolman, 1976:184). In discussing family origin material in supervision, clearly the emphasis is on the therapeutic person. The question remains whether this is the most efficient way to learn to do therapy. Some theorists have placed more emphasis on the therapeutic modality and context. Their focus has been on exposure of therapist interventions and technique (Wolman, 1976:185). Any therapy supervision that fails to integrate all three components will be necessarily limited in utility (Budman, 1981: 420-422). Haley goes so far as to say that self-expression of the client (and in the framework of this article, or therapist) cannot be separated from the context of the therapy (Greenwald, 1967:208). For the use of family of origin material to be effective in treatment and supervision, this is a basic point that is paramount. Family of origin material in supervision is relevant in the context of other questions, such as: What are the problems that face the family? What techniques are most appropriate in dealing with family problems? What are the goals of the treatment? How will outcomes be measured and evaluated? How will therapist "blind spots" be identified and overcome? Only within the framework of these questions and other similar questions will family of origin material ultimately benefit, help, and be useful to the therapist.

Visualization of family of origin material is one way to explore family of origin material for the worker. A number of effective visualization techniques in supervision such as live supervision, videotape, role play, one-way mirrors, etc. (see: Blumenfield, 1982: 93-95; and Munson 1983:219-237) have been developed and can be appropriately adapted to FOO-focused supervision. The decision as to whether the thoughts and feelings fostered by the images are verbalized should remain under the control of the supervisee.

How much material is revealed about one's family of origin should remain under the control of the supervisee and not the supervisor. To pressure supervisees to confront their own family of origin material distorts the learning process in supervision. Effective use of family of origin material can be learned and used in treatment without experiencing intensive family of origin groups by the therapist. Fontane (1979) has clearly articulated the use of such techniques in marriage counseling. Fontane makes the point that couples in therapy should not be pushed to uncover family of origin material they are not ready to deal with (Fontane, 1979:535). This same rule should apply to therapists who undergo family of origin groups as part of their learning. This is important because there is a tendency to require activities or have expectations of practitioners that go beyond what patients are expected to do simply because they are therapists. The supervisor who presses the supervisee beyond points that he or she is comfortable with, must ask why he or she is persisting in such a course of interaction.

To guard against such a distortion of the supervisory learning experience, a good policy of the supervisor should be to explore family of origin material only after case material has been presented and problem areas in the case identified. The general rule being proposed here is that exploration of patient dynamics should always precede exploration of therapist dynamics in the supervision. Through such a policy it is always assured that the supervision will remain learning focused, and at any point the therapist is reluctant to go further with his or her personal material, the therapist can fall back on the case material. When family of origin material of the therapist is the exclusive focus of the supervision, the therapist can feel trapped when he or she reaches a point he or she does not want to go beyond.

In summary, an old observation by N. Northcote Parkinson (1957) is a quite fitting analogy for use of family of origin material in supervision. He cautioned that "the patient and the surgeon should not be the same person."

REFERENCES

Beck, Robert L., "Process and Content in the Family of Origin Group," *International Journal of Group Psychotherapy* 32 (April 1982a), pp. 233-244.
————, "Teaching Family Systems Theory: A Group Experience in the Field," November 1982b, Mimeographed, Baylor College of Medicine, Department of Psychiatry.
Bissell, LeClair *et al.*, "The Alcoholic Social Worker: A Survey," *Social Work in Health Care* 5 (Summer 1980), pp. 421-432.
Blumenfield, Michael, *Applied Supervision in Psychotherapy,* New York: Grune and Stratton, 1982.
Bowen, Murray, *Family Therapy in Clinical Practice,* New York: Jason Aronson, 1978.
Braverman, Shirley, "Family of Origin as a Training Resource for Family Therapists," *Canadian Journal of Psychiatry* 27 (December 1982), pp. 629-633.
Budman, Simon H. (ed.), *Forms of Brief Therapy,* New York: The Guilford Press, 1981.

Carter, Elizabeth, and McGoldrick, Monica, *The Family Life Cycle: A Framework for Family Therapy*, New York: Gardner Press, 1980.

Fisch, Richard et al., *The Tactics of Change: Doing Therapy Briefly*, San Francisco: Jossey Bass, 1982.

Fontane, Arlene S., "Using Family of Origin Material in Short-Term Marriage Counseling," *Social Casework* 60 (November 1979), pp. 529-537.

Goldenberg, Irene, and Goldenberg, Herbert, *Family Therapy: An Overview*, Monterey, California: Brooks/Cole Publishing Company, 1980.

Greenwald, Harold (ed.), *Active Psychotherapy*, New York: Atherton Press, 1967.

Gurman, Alan S. (ed.), *Questions and Answers in the Practice of Family Therapy*, New York: Brunner/Mazel Publishers, 1981.

Haley, Jay, *Problem Solving Therapy: New Strategies for Effective Family Therapy*, New York: Harper Colophon Books, 1976.

Kramer, Charles H., *Becoming a Family Therapist: Developing an Integrated Approach to Working with Families*, New York: Human Sciences Press, 1980.

Langs, Robert, *The Psychotherapeutic Conspiracy*, New York: Jason Aronson, 1982.

Magee, James J., "Integrating Research Skills with Human Behavior and Social Environment: Assessing Historical and Cultural Influences on Students' Family Structure," *Journal of Education for Social Work* 18 (Winter 1982), pp. 14-19.

Munson, Carlton E., *An Introduction to Clinical Social Work Supervision*, New York: The Haworth Press, 1983.

Parkinson, N. Northcote, *Parkinson's Law and other Studies in Administration*, Boston: Houghton Mifflin Company, 1957.

Sobel, Dava, "Psychotherapy from A to Z," *Houston Post* (Sunday, November 16, 1980), p. 3.

Thistle, Pamela, "The Therapist's Own Family: Focus of Training for Family Therapists," *Social Work* 26 (May 1981), pp. 248-250.

Wolman, Benjamin B. (ed.), *The Therapist's Handbook: Treatment Methods of Mental Disorders*, New York: Van Nostrand and Reinhold Company, 1976.

Supervision of Marriage
and Family Therapy:
A Family of Origin Approach

Howard Protinsky
James F. Keller

ABSTRACT. The authors present a personal growth model of supervision that is currently being used in the doctoral program in marriage and family therapy at Virginia Tech. The model is based upon the family of origin concept of Murray Bowen. The major assumption is that as the supervisee understands and identifies various family of origin patterns that serve to inhibit his/her therapeutic effectiveness he/she can then interrupt such automatic patterns and increase personal effectiveness as a clinician.

There is evidence that marriage and family therapy supervisees who attempt to increase their self awareness and therapeutic use-of-self in the clinical setting progress more rapidly in becoming adept in clinical work than those who do not (Kerr, 1981). Hart (1982) has proposed the personal growth model as one of the three basic models of supervision and has written that most supervisors would agree that clinicians need to be insightful about self within the clinical context. However, he does point out that while most supervisors would agree with the above, there has been little written as to how this type of supervision should be carried out.

Howard Protinsky, Ph.D., is an Associate Professor of Marriage and Family Therapy at the Center for Family Services at Virginia Polytechnic Institute and State University, Blacksburg, Virginia 24061. James F. Keller, Ph.D., is a Professor of Marriage and Family Therapy and Director of the Graduate Training Program in Marriage and Family Therapy, Center for Family Services, Virginia Polytechnic Institute and State University, Blacksburg, Virginia 24061.

A personal growth model developed by the authors from the work of Murray Bowen (1978) is currently being used in the doctoral program in marriage and family therapy at Virginia Tech. It is recognized that although trainees are carefully screened and those accepted into the program are at a relatively high level of personal functioning, they will still encounter situations in therapy that arouse thoughts, feelings and behaviors that may be therapeutically counter productive. The purpose of this supervisory approach is similar to the purpose of the Personal Growth model proposed by Hart (1982); that is, to increase the supervisees' insight and emotional sensitivity by examining their interpersonal patterns that exist beyond their therapeutic relationships with clients. The intent is not therapeutic in that the emphasis is upon developing insight and sensitivity not to resolve the interpersonal problems of the supervisee.

A major part of the supervision process involves increasing the supervisee's awareness of the patterns of interpersonal behavior that were learned in his/her family of origin. It is assumed that these patterns will be repeated by that supervisee in many of his/her interactions with clients, supervisors and peers in training. Through the use of the genogram (Pendagast and Sherman, 1977), part of the supervisory process focuses on understanding the origin of these patterns. However, the major emphasis is upon how these patterns are re-enacted in the therapeutic and supervisory contexts.

Once the supervisor becomes aware of these patterns, he/she can develop certain strategies or operating principles that can be used to interrupt and dissolve such habitual modes of interaction. In the Bowenian sense, the intellectual or cognitive system of the supervisee can become operative to modify his/her behavior which in turn disrupts the previous automatic cycle of interaction. The supervisee becomes more of an actor and less of a reactor.

The cornerstone of this method of supervision is that of understanding the process of triangulation as conceptualized by Bowen (1978). For Bowen, the triangle, or three person emotional relationship system is the basic building block of any type of emotional system. Within a relationship system, the triangle is the smallest unit of interaction that is stable. Thus, a two person relationship system will move into the triangulation process when anxiety is sufficiently high. Over time in the family of origin, the triangulation patterns become repetitious, and the triangle becomes fixed. Then, the members of the family relationship system relate to each other in predictable roles.

In supervision, when something about the therapeutic situation triggers anxiety in the supervisee, he/she is then likely to react with the same patterns of triangulation that he/she experienced in the family of origin. Thus, understanding the significant triangles of the supervisee's family of origin will lead to insight into the predictable patterns of interpersonal behavior that the supervisee is likely to engage in when anxiety is present in the therapeutic system. This understanding is especially important if one operates from the Bowen Theory belief that the therapist should remain objective within the family therapy setting and, therefore, must operate from a detriangled position. Without an understanding of his/her triangulation patterns, the supervisee will more likely become fused into the family system and lose objectivity.

Fogarty (1978) stated that if the behavior of three people around any particular anxiety issue is predictable then triangulation is occurring. When that happens, the behavior of each person in the triangular relationship is determined by emotional reactivity rather than by objective thinking. In order for the supervisee to ascertain triangles within his family of origin, the supervisor and the supervisee look for repetitive patterns around anxiety issues. For example, if around the issue of dating, father always sides with his daughter against mother whom they perceive as being too strict, then this indicates triangulation.

Once the major triangles within the family of origin have been identified, then the next step is to focus on the predictable behaviors that result. Fogarty (1979) has identified one standard method for understanding a person's manner of operation within a triangle—the pattern of pursuit and distance. Fogarty has stated that a basic assumption of systems theory is that all people want closeness. As two people move toward each other, intensity often leads to fusion followed by distance. One person typically adopts the role of the pursuer who moves to fill self from others. The other adopts the role of the distancer who moves away to protect his/her space. Everyone has parts of the pursuer and the distancer within himself/herself. These are not permanent qualities, rather their activation depends upon the interpersonal context. One can be a pursuer around a certain issue with a certain other and be a distancer around another issue or person. Also, both parties in a relationship may switch pursuer and distancer roles at various points in time.

An example from clinical supervision is one supervisee's parental triangle that operated in times of anxiety in such a way that the supervisee would move toward his mother and distance from his father at times when marital conflict was present. The specific form of movement toward mother was supportive in nature, and the distancing from father was hostile. Over time, a coalition of mother and son was formed against father. Father invariably became the victimizer who was blamed for the marital stress while mother was seen as the victim who needed rescuing. Through the supervisory process, it was discovered that this triangular pattern was repeated in marital therapy whenever the conflict between spouses in the session reached a level intense enough to create anxiety for the supervisee. He would then move to support the wife against the husband. This side taking was carried out through verbal support, through his body posture favoring the wife and through his inability to see both sides of the conflict.

Another way of understanding the pattern of interaction within the triangulation process is through the identification of the interpersonal style of the over-functioner and under-functioner (Burden, 1980). Over-functioning is a form of pursuit in which a need is perceived in another, and the pursuer acts to take care of that person. The over-functioner chooses to avoid anxiety and low self-esteem by being overly responsible for another. He/she gains a sense of adequacy by being in charge and taking care of the under-functioner. The under-functioner deals with anxiety by being one down and having another upon whom he/she can depend.

This repetitive pattern of under-functioning was seen in one supervisee's sibling triangle involving himself, his older brother and his father. Whenever he perceived that his father was making demands upon him he would adopt a position of weakness, and his older brother would then side with him against father. This process led the supervisee to adopt a position of under-responsibility and allowed his brother to function for him at times of perceived weakness. At times during therapy when this supervisee would feel confused or stressed due to not believing he was adequate enough to handle some situation, he would adopt an under-functioning position by becoming very inactive. Sometimes the therapy sessions would get out of control during these under-functioning times, and often one family member would rescue the supervisee by taking over and offering suggestions as to what to do in the session.

The pattern of over-functioning is often seen in trainees who have a tendency to be child rescuers. They tend to see the child as a helpless victim who needs defending. This mode of operation often leads to the therapist functioning for the child in the sessions and saving the child from the perceived harsh treatment of the parents.

After an understanding is made of the origin and nature of the triangular patterns that the supervisee is likely to repeat in the therapy process, the next step is to help the supervisee become aware of the internal and external signs that indicate to him/her that past patterns are being re-enacted. This strategy is based upon the cognitive-behavioral concepts discussed by Meichenbaum (1977). The supervisee is assigned the task of reviewing his/her therapy tapes to find those sections where he/she re-enacted past triangular patterns. The supervisee then begins to identify the interpersonal cues such as the reactions of the clients to him/her and intrapersonal cues such as thoughts, feelings, images and physiological reactions that are associated with being fused into the triangulation process.

Once the signs of re-enactment have been identified, they then become defined as a stimulus not for the re-enactment of the past but for a new set of more therapeutically appropriate behaviors. Thus, this process of self-observation and identification of cues of re-enactment becomes an opportunity for the supervisee to engage in different responses of a more therapeutic nature. These different behaviors will have been discussed and rehearsed in prior supervisory sessions. For example, a supervisee who often finds herself in a power struggle with the mother and supportive of the father in a certain family would first learn what internal reactions and reactions from her client would let her know that she is again starting this process. At that point, she might notice the feeling in her stomach, her tone of voice, her body posture, and the reactions of the couple. If those signs indicate triangulation to her, she then can employ a self-management strategy previously decided upon by her supervisor. For example, she might say to herself, "I recognize that I am in the beginning stages of triangulation with this couple and I will extricate myself by focusing on the process between them and remaining neutral in my behavior toward them." She then may call upon a mental list of questions that she can ask that refocuses the session in a more therapeutic manner.

At times when the force of triangulation is particularly compelling, it may be necessary to have the supervisee leave the room. If a one-way mirror is available, the supervisee can give the couple or family a task to work on while he/she observes from behind the mirror. The added distance often helps to restore de-triangulation and objectivity.

SUMMARY

The primary assumption of this approach is that a supervisee who becomes more aware of his/her typical patterns of interaction learned in the family of origin and understands how these patterns tend to be reenacted in therapy at times of anxiety will be able to monitor those behaviors and substitute more therapeutic ones through the use of the supervision process. This process will lead to more effective interventions with clients by allowing the therapist to act more objectively in the therapeutic context.

REFERENCES

Burden, S. Tracking over-responsibility in a family sytem. *The Family,* 1980, 8, 42-45.

Bowen, M. *Family therapy in clinical practice.* New York: Jason Aronson, 1978.

Fogarty, T. Triangles. In *The Best of the Family 1973-1978.* New Rochelle, New York, 1978.

Fogarty, T. The distancer and the pursuer, *The Family,* 1979, 1, 11-16.

Hart, Gordon M. *The process of clinical supervision.* Baltimore: University Park Press, 1982.

Kerr, Michael E. Family systems theory and therapy. In A. S. Gurman and D. P. Kniskern (Eds.), *Handbook of family therapy.* New York: Brunner/Mazel, 198.

Meichenbaum, D. *Cognitive-behavior modification.* New York: Plenum Press, 1977.

Pendagast, E. G. and Sherman, C. O. A guide to the genogram family systems training. In *The Family,* 1977, 5, 3-14.

Family of Origin Work
in Systemic/Strategic Therapy Training

Bruce D. Forman

ABSTRACT. Family of Origin (FOO) tasks are discussed as an adjunct teaching tool in systemic/strategic therapy. Training procedures used to facilitate learning and applying FOO concepts are described. It is concluded that FOO work can be an integral part of training since it expands the context for doing therapy.

Since the summer of 1982 I've held a marital and family therapy (MFT) seminar as part of an informal training program affiliated with an acute psychiatric inpatient service. The purpose was to provide a group of practicing mental health professionals opportunities to enhance their skills. All trainees had varying degrees of exposure to theory through readings, workshop attendance, and coursework on MFT. Clinical supervision was formulated to comply with AAMFT membership requirements. As such, efforts were made to identify individual learning needs and devise ways of addressing them while providing a basic core of MFT material of mutual interest to all trainees. Trainees wanted to sharpen skills in working with couples and families, under supervision. In addition, each was interested in learning to effectively apply techniques stemming from the contemporary systemic and strategic practitioners, such as Haley, Minuchin, and Watzlawick.

The curriculum devised to provide trainees the opportunity to meet their expressed needs was organized similarly to that of other MFT programs described in the literature (e.g. Cleghorn and Levin, 1973; Falicov, Constantine, and Bruenlin, 1981) in terms of skill

At the time this paper was written Dr. Forman was Clinical Psychologist at the South Dakota Human Services Center, Yankton, SD. He is currently Associate Professor of Counseling Psychology, Box 248065, University of Miami, Coral Gables, FL 33124. Appreciation is extended to Steven B. Lindquist, M.S.W., and Geraldine P. Lewis, Ph.D., for their participation in training and comments during preparation of this manuscript.

levels required for MFT. These elements of the curriculum included developing observational, conceptual, and executive skills. Methods used were a combination of reading, observing MFT through a one-way mirror, participating as a co-therapist with the supervisor, receiving live supervision for ongoing MFT, and case consultation with other trainees. Philosophically, our training was quite similar to that reported by Liddle (1980), having an emphasis on systemic treatment, with an important distinction. Our program included Family of Origin (FOO) work on the part of trainees. The FOO work conducted by our trainees was grounded in Bowen's Family Systems Therapy. Despite the vast differences between Bowenian therapy and systemic/strategic therapies in tactics, techniques, and notions of what constitutes success, all rely on a general systems theory understanding. Ways in which Bowenian interpretations can be used for developing strategic interventions have been described by Berger and Daniels-Mohring (1982).

During my own preparation in MFT I participated in a geneology group, and my initial training was in a Bowenian-oriented program at the University of North Carolina School of Medicine. Bowen's Family Systems Therapy is aimed at understanding the functioning of one's family of origin and cultivating the ability to respond intellectually, in addition to emotionally, to family issues. This process is termed differentiation of self and is the primary goal of Bowenian therapy. Although I ultimately rejected the Bowenian model of therapy as not suitable in my MFT practice, I've continued the FOO work begun in 1976 along with my wife, and anticipate a long range process of differentiation. When I explained FOO to my supervisees, from a theoretical and personal perspective, I obtained consensus that FOO work would be beneficial.

PURPOSE

Each trainee came with the expectation that personal growth would be one of the outcomes of participating in MFT supervision. Inclusion of FOO work was thus consistent with their conceptions of learning. To achieve the goal of trainees' acquiring skills in applying strategic techniques, it was necessary that learners be able to conceptualize behavior systemically. Bowen's theory provided a system viewpoint based on a cybernetic model with exposure to this conception of families being valuable in understanding how system theory could be applied.

Our aim in using FOO work was to start learners considering the ways they've been influenced by their own FOO, and to recognize its potential for influencing their work as therapists. It was also viewed as a transitional device for learning how to operate within a theoretical framework different from one's own, which can be generalized to understanding how change occurs in others. Bowen's theory provided a traditional explanation of change, which then was contrasted with systemic/strategic therapy as espoused by the supervisor.

DESCRIPTION OF FOO TRAINING

Along with other elements of our training, FOO work was based on a format consistent with instructional procedures designed to maximize learning (Gagné, 1970). Elements of the learning procedure included (a) rationale for the tasks, (b) specifying the objective, (c) self-learning through reading and group discussion, (d) modeling, (e) opportunities for supervised practice, (f) immediate feedback, (g) homework assignments to assist in generalization, and (h) evaluation and correction for learning refinement. To facilitate learning and applying FOO concepts several reading assignments were made. Original sources of Bowen's work were shared among trainees (e.g. Bowen 1976; 1978). A copy of Pendagast and Sherman's (1977) "A Guide to the Genogram Family Systems Training" was distributed to each learner. This paper was useful because it delineated basic directions for constructing a genogram along with suggestions for how such could be used. A noteworthy suggestion the authors made was to identify representational systems used by family members and oneself within a Neurolinguistic Programming (NLP) (Bandler and Grinder, 1975) framework. NLP principles explain how an individual structures his/her subjective experience through auditory, visual, and/or kinesthetic encoding and decoding. The rationale for NLP methods was based partially, on systematic study of Milton Erickson's work to which Haley appealed in formulating his approach to therapy. Thus, understanding representational systems created a bridge to systemic/strategic therapy, since the family serves as an arena for learning ways of structuring subjective experience.

Trainees had other tasks in addition to reading assignments. Each was required to complete a genogram of one's own family. Only as far back as parental FOO was expected, but any available data on grandparents' FOO could also be included. Trainees' nuclear family situation was also detailed. Specific activities for genogram preparation were not limited to those suggested in the literature (e.g. Guerin and Pendagast, 1976; Pendagast and Sherman, 1977) but also came from trainee recommendations. Personal genologies were presented to peers during one of the seminar meetings. An hour or more was devoted to discussing insights gleaned from working on genograms, areas where additional work was desired, and projections for trainee's children. Trainees shared their hunches about some of the tasks which could be performed. Finally, each trainee was given the task of completing a genogram for one client or family s/he was assigned as a case. It was suggested that the case be a new one so that therapy wasn't contaminated by applying divergent treatment methods. Mixing Bowenian and strategic techniques could confuse clients about the goals of treatment and undermine therapy since markedly different strategies are involved. Finally, trainees were asked to write self-evaluations on what was obtained from completing the FOO experience.

TRAINEE OBSERVATIONS

One trainee reported that the FOO work had a continuing growth experience in professional and personal activities. It was suggested that a rapid learning about transference phenomena also took place. Thus, they discovered how their own FOO can impact in the here and now of therapy. Trainees also identified FOO work as helpful in learning how families work as systems. Below are examples of statements made in self-evaluations.

> I became aware of a communication pattern that persisted across four generations of women. I realized that I had an opportunity to differentiate myself and to support my daughters' (ages 8 and 18) processes of differentiation.

> Although I'm an only child, I discovered that only children take on characteristics of the same sex parent, based on their sibling position. My father is an oldest brother of brothers; one who tends to be in charge and in control of others. In doing family therapy my new understandings have resulted in greater ability to deal with situations wherein a family member is at-

tempting to take control. I no longer take this as a direct affront and can keep from getting embroiled in a battle. Also, understanding my sense of being "special," as an only child does, allowed me to give up a need for deference by the family and lets me shift roles more easily.

In attempting to modify relationship patterns in my FOO I learned how the homeostasis works to prevent change. I learned first hand that when change occurs it begins when the system is unstable.

After starting FOO work the next visit to my parents was dramatically different. When they began a minor argument I was able to keep out of it even though I felt an emotional pull. On the way home my spouse and I realized it was the most enjoyable visit in years.

SUPERVISOR OBSERVATIONS

Using FOO work in training systemic/strategic therapists was undertaken as a field experiment. Although Liddle (1980) points to the advantages of having learning methods consistent with theoretical aspects of MFT, there is much to recommend diverse methods within the learning paradigm. One of the most cogent features is that people can learn in different ways.

Flexibility cannot be taught directly. Yet, systemic/strategic therapists recognize the importance of options in both conducting therapy and in client's lives. This reflects the cybernetic law of Requisite Variety. Flexibility can be built in the training by requiring learners to shift conceptual sets or frames and thereby modify their context for conducting therapy. The merger of differing theoretical viewpoints need not mean that the learning of therapy models be superficial or that learning goals be vague. Certainly, the curriculum ought to focus on mastery of a therapeutic system. Familiarity with alternate modes of thinking about behavior and the language used within the various systems enables trainees to talk more easily with therapists and administrators, in addition to clients. Exposure to Bowenian methods of treatment demonstrates for trainees the possibility of client directed change within a system model of the family so that there is a recognition of system integrity (Carter,

1982) while understanding that past influences on current behavior are part of the system.

Inclusion of FOO work allows trainees to identify the blind spots which could interfere even with systemic/strategic therapy. Thus, FOO work enhances personal growth and integration of the therapist. Not only are these consistent with learner expectations for training but they are perceived as valuable and enjoyable.

REFERENCES

Bandler, R. and Grinder, J. *The structure of magic I.* Palo Alto: Science and Behavior Books, 1975.

Berger, M. and Daniels-Mohring, D. The strategic use of "Bowenian" formulations. *The Journal of Strategic and Systemic Therapies,* 1982, *1,* 50-56.

Bowen, M. Theory in the practice of psychotherapy. In P.J. Guerin (Ed.) *Family therapy: Theory and practice.* New York: Gardner Press, 1976. Chapter 3, pp. 42-90.

Bowen, M. *Family therapy in clinical practice.* New York: Jason Aronson, 1978.

Carter, E. Rapport and Integrity for Ericksonian practitioners, In J.K. Zeig (Ed.) *Ericksonian approaches to hypnosis and psychotherapy.* New York: Brunner/Mazel, 1982, Ch. 4, pp. 48-57.

Cleghorn, J.M. and Levin, S. Training family therapists by setting learning objectives. *American Journal of Orthopsychiatry,* 1973, *43.* 439-446.

Falicov, C.J., Constantine, J.A., and Breunlin, D.C. Teaching family therapy: A program based on training objectives. *Journal of Marital and Family Therapy,* 1981, *7,* 497-505.

Gagne, R. *The conditions of learning.* New York: Holt, Rinehart and Winston, 1970.

Guerin, P.J. and Pendagast, E.G. Evaluation of family system and genogram. In P.J. Guerin (Ed.) *Family Therapy: Theory and Practice.* New York: Gardner Press, 1976, Chapter 26, pp. 450-464.

Liddle, H.A. On teaching contextual or systemic therapy: Training content, goals and methods, *American Journal of Family Therapy,* 1980, *8,* 58-69.

Pendagast, E.G. and Sherman, C.O. A guide to the genogram family systems training. *The Family,* 1977, *5,* 3-14.